easy-to-use
shamanism

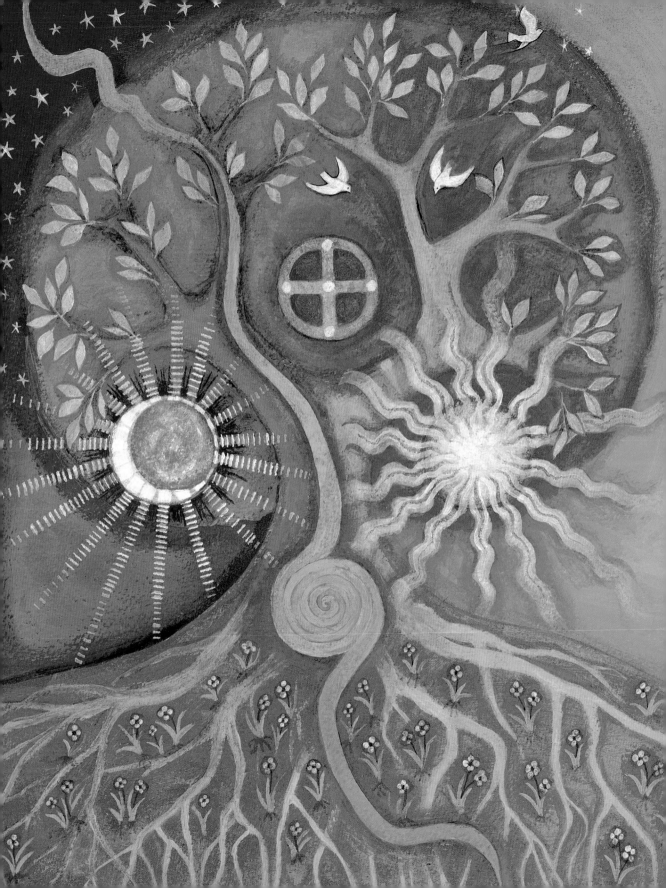

easy-to-use
shamanism

jan morgan wood

Unlock the power
of earth magic to
transform your life

vega

ISBN: 1-84333-611-1

British Library Cataloguing-in-Publication Data: A catalogue
record for this book is available from the British Library

First published in Great Britain in 2002 by
Vega
64 Brewery Road
London N7 9NT

A member of **Chrysalis** Books plc

Visit our website at www.chrysalisbooks.co.uk

Project Editors: Clare Churly and Claire Wedderburn-Maxwell
Editor: Mandy Greenfield
Designer: Liz Wiffen
Indexer: Isobel McLean

Colour reproduction by Classic Scan PTE Ltd, Singapore
Printed by Craft Print International Ltd

Contents

Introduction

Some years ago I discovered the practices of shamanism and the Medicine Wheel, ancient perspectives on life that made sense and really worked for today's world. Shamanism reaches beyond dogma, religion or prescribed beliefs and offers a complete picture of the amazing Creation we find ourselves in. This essentially animistic view of life is that everything in Creation is alive and has spirit and that all things form a Web of Life, an ever-changing flow of connection and balance. In this process every one of us forms a unique and important link with a duty of respect to all beings. It is a very wide Circle of Life in which we are all related.

Throughout our life we are constantly weaving new learning and experience into this Web of Life. When we become attuned to this process of weaving we may sense the presence of a creative and infinite guiding force. This presence has been called by many names throughout time – Atum, Vishnu, Ungud, Lesa, God – but perhaps the one that I find most accurate, which comes from Native American traditions, is the Great Mystery. By its universal nature this force defies definition and goes far beyond the boundaries of cultures and creeds. It is therefore referred to throughout this book simply as Spirit. Where mention is made of the specific non-physical or invisible aspects of earthly creation these are referred to as 'spirit helpers', 'spirit realms', 'plant spirits' and so on, or by the general term of 'spirits'.

Shamanic knowledge comes from the accumulated wisdom of worldwide cultures that have lived in harmony with the earth for countless generations; it is traditionally passed on through myths, song, dance, personal ritual and communal ceremony and celebration. Many of the teachings that form the basis of this book come especially from the ancient wisdom of the Native American peoples. These include the teachings of the Medicine Wheel, an ancient map showing how the Web of Life operates around us and within us. This map is a constant source of guidance and advice for all aspects of our being – heart, mind, body and spirit. There is an opportunity here to explore how it works through the four elements: water, air, earth and fire.

A shaman is a healer, visionary and soul doctor who 'walks between the worlds' of the everyday and spirit realms, the visible and invisible, with the aid of special spirit helpers. His or her training is long, demanding and involves practising highly specialized skills. It is not a course with a certificate at the end, and no book could train you to become a shaman. But you can begin to explore the world shamanically – to connect with the visible and invisible aspects of the natural world and to find your own special helpers and totems. You can begin to develop your shamanic senses, whether in a city centre or in wild places, and watch the Web in action all around you. The practical tasks, rituals and ceremonies within the book offer a way to build this foundation of personal experience and help you take these first steps to the practice of shamanism. By following this step-by-step sequence of development you can experience shamanic awareness throughout all aspects of your being – not just through the understanding of the mind but also through the actions of body, inspiration of the spirit and, most importantly, the caring of the heart. There are processes to heal, nourish and protect your own sacred self – often battered and neglected in today's haste and pressures and to honour, enrich and celebrate your life and relationships.

Always remember that your personal quest for connection and balance is also a blessing and gift to 'all our relations', spreading out into the Web of Life like ripples in a pool.

Jan Morgan Wood

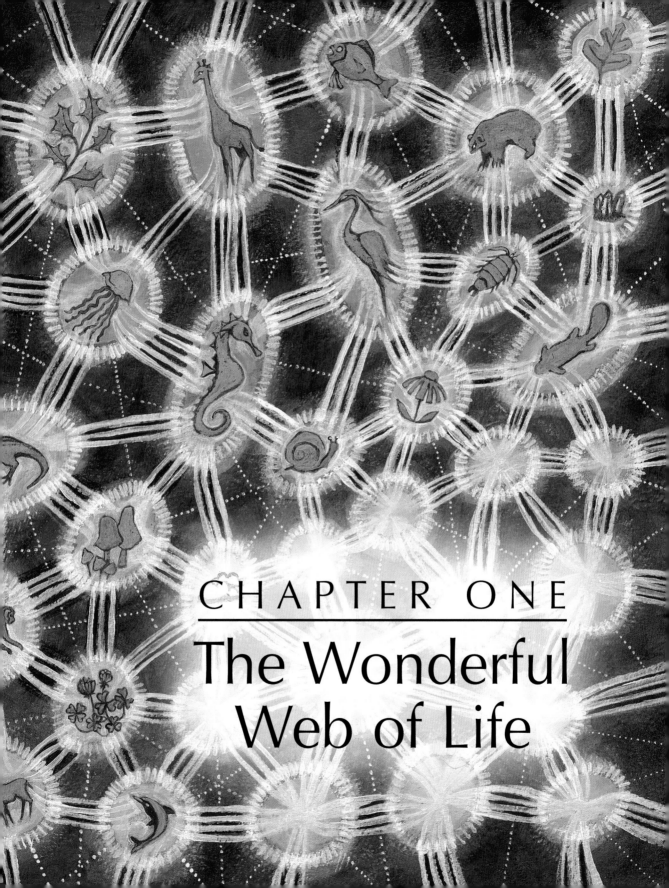

CHAPTER ONE
The Wonderful Web of Life

Our shamanic roots

Keeping a record

- Understanding often comes with hindsight, so record your experiences in a journal in as much detail as you can and read over it often to see if you can spot any repeating patterns.
- This is *your* 'earthwalk' and you are the best person to interpret your experiences, although sharing with others who understand may shed light on it for you.
- Pay attention to the way other people respond to you, for they act as mirrors of your own change. You may be told that you 'look different' or you may find others treating you differently.

The essence of shamanism is that everything in Creation is alive and interconnected in a wonderful and ever-changing Web of Life. We are related to all parts of Creation: to the four-legged ones, the stone people, the tree people, the winged and finned ones, the invisible spirits of water, earth, air and fire … When we forget our connection to the Web of Life, we experience emptiness, 'dis-ease', stress and a lack of fulfilment; when we remember our place in the Circle of Life, we feel a great sense of coming home, which is both healing and empowering.

It is often hard to feel this connectedness when our environment is of concrete and tarmac streets or when we spend much of our day in a double-glazed, insulated container. We may even lose touch with the natural rhythm of the seasons when we can buy food from all over the world at any time of the year.

The ways to reconnect with, and strengthen, our natural roots are often deceptively simple and practical. Shamanism is not an intellectual study but something that needs to be experienced physically. After all, the Web of Life is not an idea but a physical reality.

First-hand experience of these natural links brings a sense of the sacred nature of life and the fundamental principle of any shamanic tradition – respect. When we deepen our heart connection and our natural relationship with the world around us we begin to realize how closely we are related to a stone or a blade of grass. Out of this realization grow the practices and insights of shamanism.

Tuning the senses

You can begin by getting your receiving equipment in good order! The senses (including the so-called 'sixth sense' of psychic awareness that is so important in shamanism) are usually set to receive a limited waveband of information. We simply stop noticing what is not relevant to our everyday needs and tasks.

Begin to exercise your senses in ways that are enjoyable: taste unfamiliar food; concentrate your hearing to see how many different sounds you can detect in a minute; wake up your fingertips to the feel of different textures around you. When you go into nature – whether it is a park, the back garden or wild places – expand your senses to hear the sacred dialogue that is always going on. We all tune in to the messages around us according to our own skills and gifts. The key is to notice everything and censor nothing. A snail is just as likely to speak with you as a deer; a plant may attract you with its beauty, scent or thorns; a stone by offering you a place to sit. Gusts of wind or changes in the weather – even a jet roaring overhead – all these are part of the picture and should be noticed.

Exploring by doing

Ritual is the outward expression of inner meaning, the enacting of sacred purpose. The exercises and rituals throughout this book are aimed at expanding your awareness in a shamanic way and at exploring the unseen world of energies and natural spirit helpers of the shaman. Simplicity and a sense of sacred play are the keys to carrying out the processes described here. Enjoy what you do: let the deep wonder of a child fill your senses; savour the natural sounds around you or play gentle, calming music; burn incense or add flowers to decorate the place you are in.

Flexibility and humour

Be creative and adapt the rituals to your own situation, resources and surroundings. Be kind with yourself, for there is no competition and no ideal way of 'getting it right'. Let the support of the elements and the spirits around you enfold and guide you. Honour your needs and allow space for them, and keep a sense of humour – shamanism is not always solemn. If I begin to take myself too seriously or get overly anxious about how 'well' I am doing a ritual, Spirit will soon gently remind me to get my feet back on the ground, with a stubbed toe, a bird blessing on my head or perhaps an attack of hiccups!

Touching the earth

This ritual is so simple that you can do it any time, anywhere, to focus and connect with the Web of Life, as well as before and after any sacred work.

1 Bend down and touch the earth with your hand and pause for a moment to feel the presence of Mother Earth and Father Sky and all your relatives in Creation.

2 Say 'For all my relations' and send thoughts of love and balance to the whole Web.

3 Stand up again, take a deep breath and focus your senses on what lies around you. You may find that in that instant the Web gives a response of some kind: the cry of a bird, a stirring breeze.

Sacred ethics

- When using a space for sacred work, make sure you get permission from the property owners and others who live there.
- Ask the place you wish to use for its permission to do so. If you get a strong negative feeling, respect this, thank the place and find somewhere else. (This kind of refusal is rare.)
- Avoid using established sacred sites such as stone circles or holy wells as they have strong and potentially confusing energies.
- Offer the blessings of your sacred work to the whole Web with the words 'For all my relations'.
- Remember everyday safety precautions.
- Leave the space you have used tidy and with a blessing for those who come after you.
- Make sure you feel focused and grounded after your sacred work.
- Use natural bio-degradable materials in your rituals and ceremonies.

Our sacred earth family

All aspects and beings in Creation are the product of the union of energy (Father Sky) and matter (Mother Earth). On every level, from the scientific to mystical traditions, this is how things are.

The following simple ritual celebrates our direct kinship with Mother Earth and Father Sky, our sacred parents in this wide earth family, and hence with all our natural brothers and sisters throughout the Web. This relationship is not like the ones on a human level with our birth parents and siblings; our sacred parents can be trusted to offer us endless support and wisdom if we choose to keep in touch with the 'sacred' within ourselves and the world around us.

Greeting your sacred parents

You will need: a few stones; a candle and matches; if you are doing this indoors, use a tray of sand or soil as your piece of 'ground' to work on.

1 Find a quiet and undisturbed place (indoors or out) where you can be alone and can see the earth and sky.

2 Lay the stones in a mound or circle to represent Mother Earth. Pause and expand your senses to make a connection with the physical world all around you that is your Mother Earth.

3 Place your candle in the centre; fire represents Father Sky. Pause and look up at the sky. Sense through your imagination the presence of invisible energies weaving throughout Creation.

4 Touch the earth.

5 Light the candle, sit beside it and, speaking aloud, greet your sacred parents. It soon becomes natural to converse aloud like this. You might like to ask your sacred parents to help you to:
- Treat all your relations in Creation with respect;
- Trust your life's learning path, even when times are hard;
- Walk in beauty through your life (see page 17), wherever it takes you.

Speak naturally, using everyday language; say anything else that comes into your heart without censoring or judging it. Stay aware of what is happening around you, so that you listen to the Web of Life.

6 Blow out the candle and end with the phrase 'For all my relations'.

7 Touch the earth with both hands, sending out thoughts of harmony and love.

Cleansing and protecting

Cedar The fragrant wood and needles are a powerful general cleanser, used worldwide for ceremonies and for healing.

The four elements are water, air, earth and fire. 'Smudging' is a simple purifying ceremony that involves all four elements: water and earth are represented by the herbs you use, air and fire in the burning process. Smudging is an important and time-honoured way to use herbal incense to cleanse places, objects and people of 'atmosphere', 'vibes', 'tension' or 'staleness' and to place a protective seal around them.

Shamans from around the world have long recognized smudging as being beneficial both in healing work and in celebrations, burning different dried herbs according to their various energy-altering properties. Some African tribes still jump through smudge-smoke before hunting and pass newborn babies through it for protection. In Britain it was traditional to drive cattle between two smudge-fires in spring to rid them of unwanted pests on all levels, and rosemary smoke was carried through a house after spring cleaning had taken place.

As you explore healing and balancing with the elements, it is important to work in a clean and tidy space.

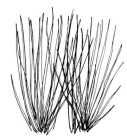

Lavender Use the flowers and stalks to sweeten and soften and to provide a cooling, relaxing energy.

When to smudge

- If there has been conflict in a room, to clear away residual emotional energy
- In a sickroom, to disperse the heaviness and to protect from infection
- If there has been a lot of mental energy exerted, such as in a planning meeting or an intensive study period

- To provide protection on a psychic level from negative or invasive energies
- To cleanse and bless food, gifts or new equipment
- To mark out the perimeter of a space for a ceremony or special sacred work.

Sweetgrass Usually supplied in long braids, sweetgrass is a reed-like plant sometimes known as 'holy grass'. It brings blessing and sweetness and is very soothing.

Smudging herbs

You can either use culinary herbs that you have purchased from a store or supermarket, or specific smudging herbs from more specialist retailers and suppliers. Alternatively, if you have a garden, why not grow your own and dry them? Herbs can be used as loose leaves or as sprigs bound together with red cotton thread in a short bundle or 'stick'.

Different plant materials give different effects. Some banish negativity, some bring sweetness, others attract positive energies and so on. To develop your own sensitivity to their properties, use two or three smudging herbs over a period of time and note how you feel before, during and after using each one. It is often easier to get to know their qualities by comparing one with another. You will no doubt develop one or two favourites and will begin to build up a small stock of herbs. As you get more experience of smudging, you can try blending two or three herbs together for different cleansing effects.

Rosemary An evergreen herb, rosemary brings gentle cleansing and sweetening, and is specially effective in the sickroom.

Common sage This herb has a bitter quality, but it is an excellent banisher of negativity.

The smudging ceremony

You will need: herbs; matches; an earthenware or heatproof dish or shell; a feather to direct the smoke and keep the herbs burning.

1 Place your herbs in the container, then light them, offering a prayer of thanks to Grandfather Fire and to all the elements present.

2 Let the flames die down until the herbs are smoking and smouldering, fanning them with your feather to keep them burning. Use the feather to direct the smoke around whatever you wish to smudge: yourself, your room and so on.

3 Allow yourself to be intuitively drawn to areas that need special attention. This will develop your inner sense of the places in particular need of cleansing. Avoid analysing this too much; just trust the smudge to guide you

Safety notes – Put containers on heatproof surfaces after use; make sure the smudge is extinguished properly; use extra care around flammable surfaces, such as bedding or soft furnishings.

Desert sage This herb from North America is often incorporated in commercial smudge-sticks and has a soft, peppery smell.

The life quest

Life is a voyage of learning for the soul, which we undertake as creatures of both spirit and matter. However, at birth, or soon after, we forget the task of learning that our soul has taken on. From then on our lessons are learned through practical experience of life itself. The path of life has many twists and turns, and we need to keep it blessed for our progress along it.

Walking in beauty

The personal resources that we find on the Medicine Path lead us towards becoming self-reliant human beings. 'Medicine' is a general term used by Native American peoples, meaning knowledge and power. We can walk this path only by finding out who we truly are; this is called 'walking in beauty'.

The exercise below is inspired by a Navajo healing prayer and blesses your past, present and future life. The energies of healing and blessing can travel – through the power of your intent – to any place or time. You do not need any qualifications or special knowledge to do this, just a clear focus.

This is your chance to give yourself this gift of blessing. Do it often – and maybe try out the different kinds of blessing methods suggested here.

Remember that when you walk in beauty, your own blessing goes out into the Web of Life like ripples in a pool, as all things are connected.

Blessing your path

1 Choose one of these blessing methods: light from a candle; the sound of a bell, drum or rattle; smoke from herbs or incense; or scattering cornmeal.

2 Find a time and place where you will be undisturbed. Take time to stand quietly and focus on the means of blessing that you have chosen.

3 Say the following words aloud, and at each * in the verse, turn to offer your blessing towards the direction you are addressing ('before', 'behind' etc.), and eventually return to face in the same direction that you began. At each point of offering, take as long as you need to feel within yourself a strong sense of blessing.

'May I walk in beauty.
With beauty before me, may I walk *
With beauty behind me, may I walk *
With beauty above me, may I walk *
With beauty below me, may I walk *
With beauty all around me, may I walk *
On a path of peace, may I walk *
May I walk in beauty.
For all my relations.'

The benefits of silence

One of the most powerful tools in the shamanic kitbag is the ability to be still, to observe the world clearly. But this is often a challenge. Even if we manage a quiet moment, the mind scurries about relentlessly, as all kinds of thoughts bubble up. We may also feel it is wrong to be 'idle' or put off our quiet time until certain tasks have been done. It may be a long wait!

I was taught the power of stillness by one medicine teacher who, when asked a question, would sit very still and 'enter the silence' to consult Spirit. It was a very focused space, not a dreamy one. The answer would come in its own time: clear and concise. Within this silence we can access wisdom far beyond our own mental processes – knowledge from within the Web. Shamans have been using this kind of sacred Internet for millennia. Through silence we can also find healing and balancing energies, without the need for special qualifications.

Of course, our ability to connect with silence varies with our circumstances, time, health and surroundings, so it is important to practise the skill as much as possible, on a regular basis, so that we can access it when we need to. Begin with just a few minutes (daily if possible) and gradually extend the time to about fifteen minutes. It will bring real benefits in vitality and clear thinking.

Entering the silence

1 Find a place and time where you will be undisturbed.

2 Sit or lie comfortably, with your spine straight.

3 Feel the weight of your body where it is supported by the chair or floor.

4 Feel your breath passing easily in and out of your body, unhurried and flowing.

5 Enter the silence and allow any thoughts to pass by like bubbles in a stream, without engaging with them.

6 When you are ready to re-enter the everyday, open your eyes and let them focus on an object near you. Feel the weight of your body, then take a deep breath. Begin to move, stretch, rub the back of your neck. Have a walk around and maybe a drink of water or some food.

The song of the earth

When you are used to entering the silence, use this exercise to explore the great song of life, the vibration of Creation. This can be done in any space that feels comfortable to you.

1 Enter the silence, as opposite.

2 Listen with all your senses to the sky, rocks, birds and creatures, plants and trees. Let them sing to you as they have sung from the beginning of time, each with their own voice.

3 When you have listened for a while, watch or listen to the vibration of your own being flowing into the Web – this is your own song.

4 When you are ready, return to reality. Take time to get back into focus, as this can be a powerful experience.

CHAPTER TWO
The Elements

A map for living

Throughout countless generations human beings have collected knowledge about the way the natural world actually works, its patterns and its energies. This knowledge has been vital to our survival, both as communities and as individuals.

The Medicine Wheel is a wonderful map of Creation drawn from ancient Native American sources. It explains the way the world around and within us connects and behaves. We can use the Medicine Wheel to help us explore and understand any aspect of life. In using it for reflection and guidance, I have been reminded again and again how effective and reliable it can be.

The Medicine Wheel looks like a compass, and by knowing the qualities of each Direction we can use it to orientate our life and loves, bringing balance, awareness and healing. The outer circle represents the circle of all life, while the inner cross reflects balance and harmony. Everything in Creation – seen and unseen – has a place somewhere on the Wheel. It charts both the outer world around us (beginning with the four elements of water, air, earth and fire) and our personal world (heart, mind, body and spirit). By working with the blessings and challenges of each Direction, we are aligning with natural energies, whose effect is gentle and energizing.

Greeting the Powers

(Facing South)
'South Power, I greet you and thank you for your blessings.'

(Turn clockwise to face West)
'West Power, I greet you and thank you for your blessings.'

(Turn clockwise to face North)
'North Power, I greet you and thank you for your blessings.'

(Turn clockwise to face East)
'East Power, I greet you and thank you for your blessings.'

Calling in the Four Directions

At each of the Directions there is a sacred energy, or Power, that holds the qualities of that Direction. Later in this chapter we will find out how to consult these Powers for guidance and help. First, let us greet the Four Directions and experience the peace and harmony that their presence can bring. While they are always present in life, by invoking them, or 'calling them in', we bring ourselves into more conscious contact and deepen our own relationship with them.

Calling in can be done daily to connect with the natural energies of the Web or before doing any kind of inner or sacred work; you can also call in at times when you feel the need for extra harmony, perhaps before a special meeting or event. See if you notice any change in the atmosphere during or after calling in. It can make quite a noticeable difference. You may wish to use a compass to align yourself precisely or make an approximate estimate.

Powers of the South: the element of water

Element: water

Quality: giving

Realm: plants

Human aspect: emotions

Human challenge: fear

Time: past

When we meet water in the everyday world – in rain running down windows, pouring down a flooded gutter or the playful tumbling of a stream – we are fully aware of its down-flowing nature. We see its persistent track as it wears away the banks of rivers until great valleys are carved through the landscape, and it can bring the activity of the world to a standstill under a silent blanket of snow. This is all part of its Medicine Power, its sacred way of being.

It is in the nature of water to flow together and find its own level. Each raindrop will meet others as they trickle over the ground into streams, rivers and eventually the great oceans that cover most of the Earth. As the oceans ebb and flow with the passage of the Moon across the sky, moisture rises and vast clouds form to ride the winds until they find a place to fall again as rain. This cycle has gone on ceaselessly throughout time, sustaining the life of the plant realm. Plants sit at the South of the Medicine Wheel and, through their gifts of nourishment, form the baseline of the food chain that supports all life. They also give shelter and medicinal herbs to many living beings, and the main quality of the South is giving.

The human aspect associated with the South is the emotions, which are akin to water in their need to flow freely. If our feelings get dammed up or frozen, or simply stagnate from restriction of movement, help is needed. Our own body mechanism for clearing out the harmful chemicals caused by emotional distress is, of course, the water of our tears.

The time quality of the South is the past, where we have accumulated most of our emotional baggage and pain. Water has an affinity with carrying memories, so it can help bear away our pain. An effective way to ask for help is to go to a river bank or bridge and speak your fears, doubts and painful memories into the water. Watch it carrying them away and know that they are being recycled in the endless flow of the water medicine. If this kind of location is not possible, you can improvise by speaking into a bowl of water and then pouring it onto the ground, or by taking a 'sacred shower' and watching the water flowing away down the plughole. Shamanic work does not depend on a perfect setting in order to be effective, as long as you know the alchemy: the energetic essence of how the element works.

The plant realm

Plants play a vital role in regulating water circulation around the planet, as roots and leaf systems pump water from the earth and release it into the sky.

Each plant has its own medicine, its part to play in the Web of Life. A plant has responses and can send messages to others of its kind over surprisingly large distances. It may also have ways of getting insects and animals to help pollinate the next plant generation, distribute seed and even provide cultivation.

Through time-lapse photography we can now see how plants dance in response to light and the seasons and observe their agility and ingenuity in finding new places to move to, despite being apparently 'rooted' to the spot. The dance of a plant may take an hour, a day or a year, and each plant has its own unique dance.

The tree dance will help you find out more about the life of a tree. You need not choose a particular species, although it may become clear to you that your tree is of a specific type. Shamans may 'dance' a plant or creature to communicate with its spirit and find out about its medicine powers.

Tree dance

You can do this in silence or use a rattle or drum, letting your intuition guide you as to speed and rhythm. There is no 'correct' way, except to follow what you feel in your heart.

1 Stand still for a few moments and, when you feel ready, greet the South Power and ask it for a teaching about trees.

2 Feel the earth supporting you beneath your feet and the sky spreading away above your head.

3 Begin to imagine what it is like to be a tree: the roots extending down into the ground, pushing between the little stones and through the earth, drawing up water and nourishment for the leaves.

4 Sense the tree's branches reaching up in search of light, drawing the sunlight's energy down through the leaves towards the roots.

5 Keep focused on the spirit of the tree that you are dancing. Continue until you sense the dance is complete.

6 Thank the South Power and the spirit of the trees.

7 Stand still and bring your awareness back to reality.

8 Feel the sky above and the weight of your feet on the earth and wriggle your toes and fingers. If you are still feeling distant, stamp your feet and clap your hands.

9 Record all that you remember of the experience in your journal.

Powers of the North: the element of air

At the North of the Medicine Wheel we find the element of air. We experience the movement of air, ranging from the merest kiss of a breeze to a howling hurricane that flattens all before it. This invisible element flows around Mother Earth in great swirls and ripples, driven by the heat of the sun above and the spinning of the earth below. We can trace its presence only by the effect it has: the flight path of a soaring bird, the dance of a falling leaf, hats being tugged off or the knife-straight line of smoke from a fire on a still day. Or we may hear the soothing sounds of a wind chime or the whining song of wind through telegraph wires.

The creatures of the animal realm also sit at the North point of the Medicine Wheel. They are the air-breathers: those who depend on breathing throughout life, from the instant of their birth. Many of them can ride the currents of the air with consummate skill – the bird nation sensing every shift of the wind through their sensitive feather structures; insects whose tiny wings beat faster than the eye can see. Some hitch a temporary ride – spiders that throw out their silken threads to catch the breeze, bats that skim through the twilight twisting and turning on their wings of skin. The realm of the creatures covers all air-breathers – even those with gills that allow them to breathe underwater.

An open mind

The human aspect of the North is the mind. Good supplies of fresh air allow the mind to perform at its best, but put someone in a stuffy room for any length of time and their brain power soon suffers. Indeed, much of the stress that builds up through overuse of our brains can be treated effectively with better breathing habits and an improved air supply. The mind is often occupied with thoughts and plans for the future, which is the time zone of the North. But the real danger comes when we believe that we have all the facts, we know what's best, the data files are closed and no more information is allowed in. Receiving is the main quality of the North, whether it is through in-breaths or through mental input. If either ceases, there is trouble!

Powers of the North

Element: air

Quality: receiving

Realm: animals

Human aspect: mind

Human challenge: closed mind

Time: future

Watching the wind

- Burn incense and 'stir' it with a stick or finger
- Blow soap bubbles over a candle and watch them catch the thermals
- Hang up wind chimes and bells
- Go outside on a windy day and have the wind as a dancing partner to guide and move you around
- Track air patterns on TV weather forecasts
- Fly a kite.

The animal realm

The initial training for a shaman often includes very practical and down-to-earth skills such as tracking, scouting and wilderness survival. These involve the ability to get close to animals in the wild and study their habits and medicine qualities without being seen. You can try this by making a 'still hunt' – an exercise in blending into the landscape and observing it in minute detail.

The ability to assume this state of invisibility can be equally useful in the urban jungle. This is the skill of the fox, a master of camouflage and silent watching. You might ask if the fox will help you learn this, or call to some other creature with which you feel affinity and which knows how to wait, watch and blend. The still hunt can be done with a special focus, but for now simply let your intention be a general one to observe how these creatures live.

Tips for still hunting

- Practise imagining that you are invisible
- Pretend that you are a leaf on a tree or a blade of grass
- Keep your attention focused on the present moment
- Keep your muscles and breathing as relaxed as possible
- Avoid wearing strong deodorants or perfume
- Choose a comfortable spot with shelter from the wind, rain and sun
- If you need to shift position, do so slowly and smoothly
- Be prepared for your creature relatives to get close
- Remember, common-sense safety: you are food to some creatures.

Still hunting

1 Choose a time and place where you will not be disturbed and that feel welcoming to you.

2 Make yourself comfortable – this is not an endurance test – and relax into the setting, becoming part of the scenery. Feel your connection with the Web of Life and wait.

3 Observe every detail of what goes on around you: the weather, insects, clouds, scents and sounds.

4 When you have finished your still hunt, leave a heartgift (see opposite) and return to everyday reality. This adjustment may take a few moments, so give yourself time.

5 Record your experiences in your journal as soon as possible.

Make a windcatcher

Celebrate the dance of the air element by making a windcatcher.

1   Find a sturdy stick at least 18 in (45 cm) long and trim any small twigs back to the main branch. You can peel off the bark if you wish. On some species of tree this is easier than on others.

2   Decorate the stick with beads, streamers and ribbons and tie on feathers, lightweight shells and other natural materials that will catch the movement of the air. Do not make the streamers too long, as they will tangle up after a while.

3   Put the windcatcher where you can watch it and try placing it in different parts of your garden, balcony or patio – stand it in a pot of earth if you don't have any spare ground.

Natural materials

- When you seek to use materials from nature, such as wood or stones, you are asking for a gift from a relative's being. Always respect this by explaining to them what you are doing and why you need them.

- Leave an appropriate token of your thanks (a 'heartgift') in the place of the materials you have used: for instance, water, birdseed, fruit or incense. Litter removal is as good a gift to leave as any, since it exchanges and balances the energy received.

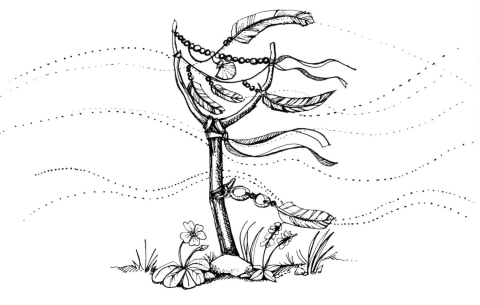

Powers of the West:
the element of earth

The West is connected to the element of earth. It is a place of solid, here-and-now physicality and is the Direction associated with our physical body.

There is a stillness and tranquillity in mountain landscapes, or on a rocky shore, that is the Medicine Power of the earth element. The quality of the West is that of holding, and the rocks and stones that form its associated mineral realm hold warmth and cold long after the temperature around them has changed.

In shamanism we use the medicine quality of earth as a holder of energy to bless, heal and balance. We also regard each stone, each grain of sand, as a living relative to be respected. Looks do not count when it comes to the power of a stone person. A quartz crystal or a perfect ruby may have great aesthetic beauty to us, but generally shamans work with far less glamorous pebbles and stones.

The Blessing Stones Trail helps us develop an awareness of the individuality of stones, how to ask them for help and how to weave positive energy into the landscape. To call to the stone people you simply state your request in a sacred manner, explaining what you need help with. You then walk out to meet them, keeping all your senses alert to discover which stone attracts you – by its colour, position or even by tripping you up! Bear energy is closely allied to the Direction of the West, so you might ask the bear to help you with this learning.

Powers of the West

Element: earth

Quality: holding

Realm: minerals

Human aspect: body

Human challenge: inertia

Time: present

Blessing Stones Trail

1 Enter the silence (see page 19) and ask to meet the stone people who wish to help you make a Blessing Stone Trail. You may want to leave a particular kind of blessing, such as peace or good luck, or simply intend a general blessing and leave it to Spirit to know what is needed in the places you connect with.

2 Begin your walk and, when you find a stone helper, pick it up with thanks and carry it in your hand, focusing on the blessing you have chosen. When it feels right, or the stone shows you in some way (by getting heavier, changing temperature or even slipping from your grasp), put it down.

3 You may find the next stone immediately or you may have to walk on a little way before you find another. When you are working shamanically, you meet Spirit halfway and let events unfold in the way that is right at that time. Whether you end up picking up one stone or twenty, this is not a reflection on how well you are doing, whether you are worthy or whether the stones like you. You have no way of knowing whether a tiny act is the quantum shift needed for some change in the Web of Life.

Building a Medicine Wheel

A stone Medicine Wheel brings positive energy to a place, as well as being a symbol of harmony that can be incorporated into a garden or the sanctuary corner of a room. We find many examples of ancient stone circles throughout the world and their purposes have largely been forgotten. But in North America there are ancient stone Medicine Wheels that are still active as sacred sites for tribal peoples. Some cover large areas and have many stones.

You will need: a compass; smudge-kit (see page 15); four stones of roughly equal size; some cornmeal or loose smudging herbs; a heartgift for the land.

1 Go to the place you have chosen and connect with it by sitting there for a while in the silence or by singing or drumming.

2 Clear the space: if you are outdoors clear any brambles, large weeds, rubbish and so on; if you are indoors clean the area and perhaps lay out a beautiful cloth or natural grass matting where the Wheel will be laid out. Using the compass, find out where East lies in relation to the space.

3 Smudge yourself, the stones and your sacred area.

4 Look at your stones and intuitively choose which Direction each will represent.

5 Place each stone in turn at its Direction on a pinch of smudge or cornmeal saying:
'I invite the blessings of the East Power to be here in beauty and balance.
I invite the blessings of the West Power to be here in beauty and balance.
I invite the blessings of the South Power to be here in beauty and balance.
I invite the blessings of the North Power to be here in beauty and balance.'

6 Return to the East of the Wheel and give thanks to the Powers and the spirits of the place and leave your heartgift (indoors this may be an offering of quiet music, incense or a lit candle).

Earth riding

We travel through the Cosmos of Creation on a galactic voyage, riding on Mother Earth. She dances her way around the sun, just as our sun circles around myriad others, in a beautiful and complex weaving of light and form.

Take an 'earth ride' whenever you need a quiet space in which to regain a sense of proportion in your daily life, or when you need to heal, recharge your batteries and touch base with sacred reality.

1 Find a time and place where you can lie down undisturbed. Lie on your belly and relax, letting your breath flow deep into the earth, feeling the beat of your blood and the weight of your body as you lie heart-to-heart with Mother Earth.

2 If there is any physical, mental, emotional or spiritual pain that you want to release from your being, let it flow away into the ground, to be recycled as pure energy. Feel the support and nourishment that has been there throughout your life. Let yourself be nourished now in whatever way you need and give Mother Earth a hug of thanks.

3 When you are ready, sit up slowly and take all the time you need to refocus on your surroundings.

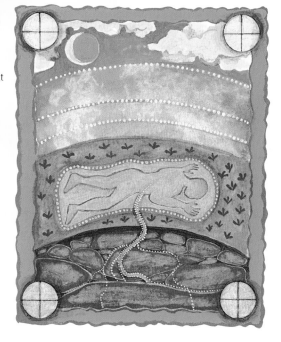

Power of the East: the element of fire

Fire has mystery and immense power. The flames of a fire or a candle constantly move skywards. And where do they go? Looking at their tips, we see light and energy trailing into nothing. So fire is associated, on the Medicine Wheel, with the non-physical aspect of our being – the unseen inner qualities by which we can make changes, determine courses of action and follow our personal vision. But we must beware of wandering too far off into the realms of imagination; we can find this place of fantasy very seductive and be loath to keep in touch with reality.

A powerful cleanser and an awesome force, fire can level buildings and forests or can provide the warm hearth around which we love to gather. No wonder it has long been equated with transformation and with the carrying of our prayers and requests into the spirit dimension. It is associated with all time and with the realm of humans. In this fire-lighting exercise you can celebrate your spirit aspect and invite the fire to visit you. If you do not have suitable space outdoors, it can be done inside using an indoor hearth or candles.

Powers of the East

Element: fire

Quality: transformation

Realm: humans

Human aspect: spirit

Human challenge: illusion

Time: all time

Making a sacred fire

You will need: enough stones to encircle the fire; smudge-kit (see page 15); dry twigs and grass or candles.

1. Smudge the area, yourself and the stones. Set the stones out in a circle where your fire is to be made.

2. Make a pyramid-shaped pile of dry twigs and grass inside the stones and place some smudging herbs in the centre with prayers inviting Grandfather Fire to come and sit with you for a while.

3. Light the kindling (or candles) from the East. Fan if necessary to get the fire going. This is where you find out if you have laid it well. Remember that fire travels upwards, so light at the base and feed it extra twigs as needed.

4. Now sit and fire-gaze. Let the flames speak to you through their patterns, their song and the curling smoke. Enter a dreaming space and let Grandfather Fire warm and nourish you.

5. When you are ready to finish, thank Grandfather Fire and the stone, tree and plant people for their help. Make sure that the fire is in a state that is safe to leave (if necessary, extinguish it with water or earth). Leave the area tidy.

Safety notes – Respect personal and environmental safety; remember that lighting a fire outdoors is often regulated by law, for good reason; make sure that the spirit of the land you use is willing to have a fire lit, perhaps by making an exploratory visit first.

Purifying fire

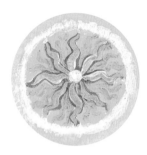

A candle can be used as an alternative to smudging with herbs. This is especially useful when the smell of herb smoke may be inappropriate. As you light the candle, give thanks to the fire for its gifts and ask that it helps you in the particular cleansing task that lies ahead. Then present the candle to each of the Four Directions, starting with the East. Use the candle flame exactly as you would the smudge smoke, passing it around the space, person or object to be purified. Your inner sense will tell you if it needs to be blown out when you have finished or can be left to burn out safely. I find that stones and crystals seem to benefit particularly from this form of cleansing.

A ceremony for healing and change

In many traditions fire plays a central role in meetings and ceremonies, with the lighting of a special fire often signalling the beginning of a community council or celebration. In South America offerings of food and flowers are made to fire in the Inca tradition, and the ashes are later 'read' and interpreted by the shaman or *inti*.

The ceremony described opposite is of Inca origin, but has been found in similar forms throughout many cultures and times. It is a ritual for releasing our wishes and hopes, our fears and burdensome issues. We offer all these things to the sacred fire, as supplicants, acknowledging that we do not always know what is best, but asking for healing and balance. We ask that those things that we want, and that Spirit knows is right for us at this time, will come to us and that we may be released from our pain, anger, sicknesses and fears, if it is right for us.

These 'lists' of requests need to be fairly short and true to what comes to us in the sacred space of the ceremony. Often the unexpected things that we find appearing on our lists are an important part of the ceremony's learning process. A short list is easier to focus on and to remember when it is time to give it to the fire.

There is no issue that cannot be brought to Grandfather Fire in this way. You can ask for that car you need, for physical or emotional healing, for a successful visit abroad or for food for your family. In my experience this ritual really works, so ask carefully!

Fire ceremony

You will need: a candle and matches; a heatproof container; smudging herbs; paper and pen.

1 Set up your space with a candle in the centre and a heatproof container to the West of the candle, with a small amount of smudging herbs in it. Smudge a circle about 6 ft (2 m) in radius from the candle.

2 Sit to the South of the candle, holding paper and a pen. Enter the silence (see page 19) to bring focus to your heart and prepare yourself to find out what lies within it at this time.

3 Write a short list of what you wish to get rid of in your life and another list of what you wish either to attract or to strengthen. Use your inner sense to guide you and take no longer than five minutes over this.

4 Watch the candle flame for a few minutes to reflect on

fire's transforming power. When you feel the moment is right, get up and move clockwise to sit by the container in the West. Light your lists from the candle, place them in the container and allow them to burn away completely.

5 Give thanks to Grandfather Fire and draw your fingers three times through the air above the candle flame, placing your fingertips in turn on your forehead, your heart area and your belly.

6 Get up and circle the candle clockwise to return to your original sitting place in the South.

7 Complete the ritual in whatever way feels right for you: perhaps in silence, by saying a prayer or singing a chant, and then blow out the candle.

Meeting the elements

The best way to meet the elements is to take a walk outside to observe them and let them speak to you. You probably have one or two preferred elements and perhaps one that you do not get on with: you may love basking in sunshine but avoid going out on a windy day; or you may hate getting wet but love collecting pebbles or crystals.

If you make this walk with a sacred intent – a Medicine Walk – you invite the unseen aspects of the landscape to make themselves more noticeable than usual. By stating your intention for the walk (in this case to meet with and learn about the elements) you send out a sacred request to the Web of Life that will help you to pick up the information you are seeking.

Medicine Walk

Preparation: decide on your starting point. This may be a doorway within your house or on the threshold; or it may be at a certain spot in nature (at a tree or bridge, the park gates, anything that is clearly tangible). Decide roughly how long the walk is to take. If you are going into wild country, tell someone reliable when you expect to return and roughly where your route will take you, as a safety precaution – ritual requires common sense too.

1 Call in the Four Directions and ask them to teach you about the elements on your walk. Then step across your starting point.

2 Proceed with your senses on full alert. If any stones, feathers or other objects call to be picked up, do so. Take in every detail and stay focused in the present moment – no daydreaming or meandering, unless it feels really right.

3 When it is time, leave a heartgift and return to your starting point and recross the line, marker or gateway.

4 Thank the Four Directions and focus again on everyday reality.

5 As soon as possible record in your journal all that you experienced, taking note of the main themes, the overall quality of the walk, how you felt at the start and finish, which creatures and plants particularly caught your attention, any unexpected or unusual happenings and so on. See if you can relate your experiences to the elements and establish what they have shown you.

6 If you have collected any natural items *en route* arrange them in your home or garden in a place where you can see them often. They are an important part of the conversation you have had with Mother Earth.

A personal Medicine Wheel

Each of us is a unique mixture of strengths – a subtle shape that is always changing as we grow and learn. This shape can be understood by looking at your characteristics on the Medicine Wheel. How do you react to a new situation? Do your feelings (South aspect) come into play first, or do you note the facts (North aspect)? Do you do something practical (West aspect) or find a creative perspective (East aspect)?

Of course every situation is different, and we respond in different ways at different times. But we do have broad preferences according to our medicine 'shape'. This shape may also be reflected in our everyday relationship with the respective elements, which could, then, be called 'strong' (for instance, 'strong earth'). You may have a strong connection with water (South) but dislike air (North). Fire (East) may alarm you, whereas you may love building rockeries and walking on pebble beaches (West).

I have mapped out some broad definitions in the following diagrams – thumbnail sketches that give an idea of how personal Medicine Wheel maps work. See where you and your friends fit in and begin to build up a picture of your personal medicine shape, finding out what aspects you need to bring into balance.

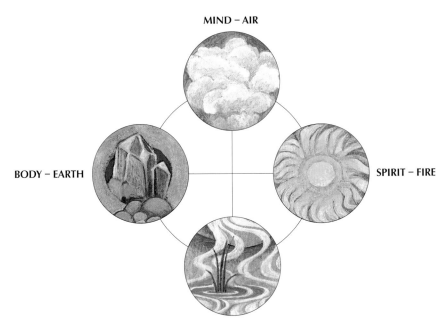

MIND – AIR

BODY – EARTH

SPIRIT – FIRE

EMOTIONS – WATER

Perfect balance: equal elements
This state of perfect equilibrium is the goal but is rarely achieved. When this balanced state is prevalent, access is gained to the energy that is usually wasted trying to cope with the imbalances in life.

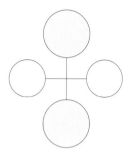

Water–air axis

Encompasses learning and awareness about the emotions (water) and thinking (air). These are often contradictory. May try to make life more manageable by polarizing the viewpoint to *either* the facts (North) *or* the feelings (South).
Positive state: openness – a flowing heart and a receptive mind.

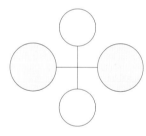

Earth–fire axis

Encompasses learning and awareness about the physical (earth) and spiritual (fire) balance within life, a sense of purpose and passion. May polarize into fantasies (East) or an overly practical and materialistic viewpoint (West).
Positive state: practicable goals and creative solutions.

Keeping the balance

The Medicine Wheel Directions relate strongly across each axis (North–South, West–East), and our life lessons at any one time tend to be related either to one axis or the other. If both elements are equally balanced, life flows and our challenges and difficulties are dealt with successfully. However, if one element predominates, the weaker opposite element will need to be worked on to achieve a balance.

For instance, someone who is equally at home with an emotional and factual response to life has a North–South balance, whereas someone who feels one thing and thinks another may be confused and flip from one side to the other. The remedy is to find out which Direction you feel strong in, or have a predisposition for, and then work on the opposite Direction, consciously acquiring the skills and attributes of the weaker aspect. For instance, if you respond from the heart (water), but have a problem tackling facts (air), life becomes limited and you need to work on breathing, being in the open, taking things in logical steps and manageable chunks. Likewise, if you prefer to think your way through everyday situations but have trouble looking at your feelings, try walking by the river, taking care of the garden or windowbox or jumping in puddles.

Sharing strengths

We sometimes make romantic or business partnerships with people of the opposite preference, in order to form a balanced operating unit between the two of us. So someone who likes to think may team up with someone who supplies the emotional aspect. This kind of symbiosis is common and can work extremely well for a while, until one person or the other begins naturally to learn the opposite skills and then the balance of the team or couple is upset. This can develop into a leapfrog situation, with each partner taking it in turns to play the role of the 'child' in the South, as the other partner moves up into the 'adult' sensible-logical position in the North. Where there is disagreement about making the swap, the couple may compete to be the emotional child or the fact-dealing parent, and conflict ensues.

Strong air

Takes time to analyse a situation and responds with logic. A good planner who can be relied on to organize.

Balance strategies: encourage curiosity in order to find what is missing from the data map. Make deliberate breaks with routine. Undertake water activities such as fishing, swimming and Jacuzzis.

Suitable careers: detective, academic, computer analyst, teacher, planner.

Strong earth

Prefers to respond to life in a practical way. Solves problems with the hands rather than the head; lives for the moment.

Balance strategies: practise active stillness through meditation or yoga and explore creativity through crafts, role-play games, music and dance.

Suitable careers: beautician, mechanic, builder, sportsman, fitness instructor.

Strong fire

Senses the spirit energy and ecstasy of life. Avoids material concerns and often experiences extremes of heat and cold.

Balance strategies: create realistic structures of time and space for expressing creative energies. Take care of yourself physically through food, sleep and exercise.

Suitable careers: musician, psychic, healer, priest/ess, natural therapist, designer, storyteller.

Strong water

Responds swiftly to life from the heart, either with open emotion or by freezing or bottling up feelings. Often caught up in issues of the past.

Balance strategies: let the feelings (especially fears) flow freely, but also take time to gather all the facts. Get outside often in the open air, practise relaxation, breathing and singing!

Suitable careers: carer, playgroup helper, counsellor, nurse, entertainer.

CHAPTER THREE

The Shaman's World

The shaman's role

The shaman establishes close working bonds with spirit helpers, who assist as the shaman travels or 'journeys' to the spirit dimensions of the Web. This journey is made during an altered state of consciousness or trance. While in the Otherworld, the shaman searches for healings, teachings or advice and may search for energies and fragments of soul that have become lost from the everyday dimension.

In this spirit dimension the normal rules of day-to-day reality are suspended, and responses to the shaman's questions or requests may come in many forms. Healing may be given via a song or by a direct transfer of energy during the journey; the location of a missing person may be shown in detail on a map; a herb or ceremony may be recommended; or a task may be set to further knowledge through practical experience. Each shaman possesses a set of skills, taught to them by other shamans and by their own spirit helpers during trance. Some shamans treat with herbs, some specialize in ceremonial healing, others alter energy through storytelling or sound.

Soul power

At birth we enter life naturally imbued with the power of our own life force – our soul essence – which holds the vitality, focus and energy that will enable us to live life to the full.

The stresses and pressures of everyday living often cause this power to drain away or fluctuate. When this power is low, we are vulnerable physically, emotionally and spiritually, and we feel separated from reality, from loved ones, from the world around or within ourselves.

A temporary boost of our personal energy can be given shamanically after illness or trauma. But when an individual's soul system has undergone extreme stress (for instance, through physical or emotional trauma, general anaesthetic, an accident or illness), part of the soul can break away – as a survival strategy – and retreat into the Otherworld dimension. Sometimes this departure is felt by the individual, but often it is not. Usually it returns naturally, but where it does not, the individual may experience loss of memory, low attention span or hyperactivity, general listlessness and feelings of disconnection with reality. Those around them often remark that someone is 'not at home' or 'not all there', or they notice that there is a far-away or blank quality to their eyes. These are all signs of 'soul loss'.

The shaman needs to 'retrieve' the lost soul parts by making a spirit journey to the dimensions where the soul parts have taken refuge.

The first shamanic step

Trance is a natural state that we experience all the time in everyday life. It excludes irrelevant parts of reality to make life simpler and more manageable. In shamanic trance we exclude the concrete world of the senses and open our perception into the spirit dimension.

We all have spirit helpers and totem (or power) animals, and actually knowing our spirit helpers is an invaluable resource, as they have a wealth of assistance and advice to offer. Over time this becomes a very personal relationship, and they can become our personal allies, our closest friends.

Natural trance

Much of our daily experience is of crowded, noisy or repetitive situations, which are likely to shift us into a light trance state. If we are unaware of this trance mechanism, we may live much of our lives feeling vague, disconnected, low in vitality and even struggling to communicate clearly. It is therefore important to keep track of any changes in our degree of focus on the world around us.

What are your personal internal signals that tell you that you have shifted consciousness? Do your eyes blur or feel heavy? Does your hearing alter, or do things seem far away?

The cross-and-circle exercise will help you develop your awareness of trance states in everyday life. The ability to move in and out of trance at will is a key tool in shamanizing.

Cross-and-circle focusing exercise

This exercise enables you to check on your own state of focus at any time. The circle symbolizes your physical body, the cross your non-physical being. When they are together you are at full attention in physical reality.

1 Imagine a cross of equal proportions within a circle a short distance away from you, at eye level. It need not be a strong visual image, as long as you have a clear sense of it.

2 Allow the cross to move slowly upwards until it is completely separate from the circle. Hold it steady there for a few moments.

3 Bring the cross slowly back down into the circle until it fits exactly and remains there. If it tends to drift, bring it back. Use imaginary padlocks if you have to!

Everyday trance situations

- Dancing to a repetitive rhythm
- Counting items on a conveyor belt
- Travelling in a crowded lift
- Driving on straight, featureless roads
- Listening to music in soft lighting
- Relaxing in the bath
- Waiting in a queue
- Walking through a familiar building
- Watching a film.

Grounding techniques

- Walking barefoot outdoors
- Eating or drinking
- Rubbing your eyes, face or back of your neck
- Wriggling your toes and fingers
- Saying your name and address aloud
- Clapping or stamping your feet.

Beyond everyday reality

What our mind focuses on creates thought-forms, which then exist in the world. It is important to recognize this, as our 'intent' is always going out into the Web of Life. And the use of intent is central to working shamanically and with ritual. Well-wishing has a very real existence in reality, as do less positive thoughts.

Ritual – the way to externalize and clarify our intent in a sacred context – is just as natural a human state as trance; we may wish someone well, cross our fingers for luck, touch wood for protection, even have a certain order of doing tasks to get a sense of safety. And, like all aspects of life, this can be taken to extremes. Balanced ritual and clear intent can extend our sense of a healthy connection with life and the sacred. However, within the Web our actions and thoughts must be ethical, or they will rebound on us in the future. A shaman has to be very aware of this law of consequences, and shamanic work should never be done on anyone else's behalf without their explicit knowledge and consent.

Guardians and portals

Places hold memories of what happens in them. Centuries after a powerful ceremony or sacred event, echoes of its energy can be found by those who have skills in this kind of detection. Repeated ceremony or activity imprints itself on a place, giving it a certain atmosphere.

The spirit realm also has tracks and territories all around. These are recognized in folklore the world over, and may be called spirit trails, fairy paths or ancestral grounds. They are often marked out and are forbidden or taboo, thereby protecting the interests of all concerned. There may well be spirit protectors or guardians at these spaces, either arising from the natural world or placed there by human intent. Some people are sensitive to these guardians and boundaries, while others need to develop an awareness of them.

I once watched three children romping happily in and out of a burial-chamber entrance, while a fourth could not get past a certain point, a large rock. Time and again he tried different kinds of approach, but it was as if an invisible barrier pushed him back each time. He was very frustrated to be left out of the game!

In places the veil between the worlds is thin, or has portals that are spirit gateways. These can be difficult places to live in as there is often a great deal of spirit activity around them, which can have a muddling effect on everyday human life. When doing sacred work we need to be aware of this interaction of dimensions. A place that feels magical or powerful may already have its own purposes, which would be confused and upset if we were to intrude without seeking permission.

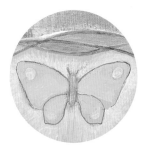

Signs of spirit boundaries

- Natural obstacles blocking your path
- Repeated distraction from your intended route
- Insects or other creatures barring your way
- A feeling of uneasiness or dizziness
- A change in temperature
- A different light quality
- A sense that time is vague or goes faster or slower than expected
- A strong perfume or distinctive scent
- A ringing in your ears or a muffling of external sounds
- Your pulse speeding up or slowing down
- The surface hairs of your skin rising up in 'goosebumps'.

Power places

We all have places that are special to us, where there may be a beautiful view, a place to sit by a tumbling stream or a sheltered corner in the garden where we can sit at twilight and enjoy the birdsong. Or we may have a favourite seat or place to look out of a window, or a cosy corner in which to listen to music by candlelight. These places restore and nourish our soul, which is so often neglected in everyday practicalities – they are somewhere we can be in touch with our core self and relax.

As we develop our shamanic awareness, it is useful to have a sacred 'power place' that exists in reality, where we can feel in deep communion with the Web of Life and with our own sacred skills. This power place forms a bridging point or gateway between this reality and the Otherworld of the spirits.

A shaman usually has at least one power place where he or she feels completely safe and comfortable – a place to meet spirit helpers, ask for healing and take time for longer periods of reflection or inner balancing work. This sacred location is also held within us, remembered in the mind's eye, as a refuge and as a source of nourishment and stability, which can be accessed with the imagination even when life is at its most hectic.

Such a power place may be in another country and visited only once or twice a year; or it may be just down the road in the park and visited every day. Sometimes it has a specific purpose: for healing, dancing or fasting. It is possible to have several power places for different purposes.

Connecting with your site

Your power place can be a refuge where you can meditate, perform shamanic rituals, meet your helpers and allies and feel your sacred position within the Web of Life. To choose your own particular place, take some quiet time to reflect on natural sites that you know, or have known well in the past, and that feel safe and welcoming. They need to be quiet and relatively free from human activity: perhaps a corner of the park or a special woodland den you had as a child. The main qualities are that it is a place in which you feel secure, happy and at home.

When you have tried out a few possibilities, settle on the one that feels easiest to connect with. Enter the silence (see page 19) and call the place to mind in more detail. What plants are growing there? What is the ground like? And where do you feel comfortable sitting within the space? Are there trees – the homes of other creatures? Are there rocks or water?

With your inner eye begin to build up a detailed awareness of the place and imagine visiting it at different times of the day, in different seasons. Do this a few times until you can summon a strong sense of the place. This process weaves it more clearly into your awareness and establishes it in the spirit realm. As you make your 'visits', be aware that this is a spirit space – your own special territory in sacred terms – and no one can enter it without your permission.

If you are able to visit the place in everyday reality, go there a few times and explore it. Take some heartgifts or pick up litter as a thanks offering. Leave some food for the creatures there. You could also pick up natural items from the site, such as stones, seeds or anything else that calls to you. Take them home and place them in a small bag or wrap them in a piece of cloth. This is a 'bundle' – a kind of shamanic link that will hold the essence of the power place for you, helping you to connect more strongly with it whenever you hold the bundle. Bundles are private possessions and are not usually shown to other people or left where others might pick them up.

If your chosen power place is outdoors, it is useful to have a second one in your home, where you are going to feel comfortable doing sacred work and are unlikely be disturbed. You can keep your bundle here, perhaps with a photograph of your outdoor site. There should be room to sit and lie down when you need to, and you should be able to switch off phones, VDUs and other equipment that emits strong electronic energy fields.

If this space has to be used by other people at different times, this does not present a problem. You simply need to find a ritual or signal that switches it on when you are using it and off when you have finished. The simpler this kind of ritual is, the better. Perhaps you could light a candle while the space is in sacred mode and blow it out to signal the switch-back. Or you could smudge before and after using the space. This also signals to your own being that you are entering a special 'inner' time and helps you to clarify the shifts in your energy and awareness.

Dancing with the spirits

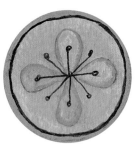

Dance and song have long been a sacred 'doorway' through which we can step into the Otherworld. The brain is readily affected by rhythm and repeated movement, which shift it into the wave patterns of trance. We have already explored this through dancing with the tree (see page 27); through the same power of imagination and intent we can find out what it is like to be animals, plant forms, clouds – even the wind; we can blend our physical being with their medicine, their sacred way of being. It is not shamanically ethical to do this in a frivolous, recreational way; we must behave as respectful visitors to the spirit realms, not as gung-ho tourists! If this respect is not shown, whatever means we use to tune in to the spirit world, we stand to be taught a lesson, have a bad 'trip' or simply be refused admission.

Song also invokes the Otherworld – especially the use of chants, which employ repetitious words and rhythms. Many traditional chants use words that are 'vocables': that is, they do not have any concrete meaning, but are sounds that are known to produce certain energetic effects and thus communicate directly with the energies of the Otherworld. These might be words like 'hey' or 'weya', which contain harmonic resonances in terms of sound-science.

Sounding your rhythm

Drum: use any type of drum or improvise with a wooden spoon and an upturned bucket

Rattle: use maracas, a gourd, hide rattles, bunches of shells or improvise with dried rice in a plastic container

Click: clap together two hardwood sticks a few inches long or two wooden spoons

Bell: use sleigh bells or tambourines with jingles

Between the worlds

If a song or dance has been done over a period of time, it becomes a strong thought-form in its own right and achieves a kind of life of its own by accumulating the intent of many performances. Someone singing or dancing it for the first time may find themselves caught up in this accumulated effect, whereas that same person using a personal or new song might have a much less powerful experience. These resonant ceremonial songs and dances are reserved in traditional societies for the initiated and are taught only when the person is ready. This may look like élitism but is, in fact, common sense.

Song and dance are used to create a sacred space in which shamanic procedures such as healing can take place. Sometimes teams of specially trained singers have to perform specific songs, according to the procedure with which the shaman is working, and must keep strictly to the set rhythm and words to ensure success. This is like constructing an invisible protective building around the shaman and patient, which exists in thought-form between the worlds of the everyday and spirit, and where the shaman and the spirits can work with maximum efficiency. Sometimes the patient also has songs and dances that must be performed or tasks they must do later to complete or give thanks for the process.

The power dance

Some shamans specialize in dancing as a means of curing and bringing vision to their communities, using their own personal power dance that expresses their sacred being and their relationship with the spirit helpers. As these helpers are often in animal form, their characteristic ways of moving may be seen in the dance movements: shamans may perform eagle dances, kangaroo dances or deer dances. Parts of the animal, such as feathers, antlers or necklaces of claws, may be used in special costumes. This incorporation of animal parts into the ritual and tools of the shaman is always done with the deepest respect and love for the animals concerned.

The dance is often accompanied by the shaman's unique power song, which has been given – like the dance steps – by his spirit helpers. This combination of dance and song sends out the shaman's call to the spirit world and links him or her to it (like tuning in to a radio frequency). The dance also reinforces the shaman's sacred identity and gifts.

Finding your own power dance and song

Having your own power dance and song is a way to celebrate your being as a child of both sky and earth. It has absolutely nothing to do with dancing, singing or musical skills. If you were told you had no talent in these directions in the past, forget it. If you can talk, you can sing; if you can move, you can dance. This is not about performance – it is about your natural connection with life.

You will need: smudge-kit (see page 15); a means of making a sound rhythm (see opposite).

1 Choose a time and place where you will not be disturbed. Your own power place is ideal, or anywhere you can an make inner connection with it.

2 Smudge or cleanse yourself and the surrounding area.

3 Start sounding a steady beat but allow this to vary as your intuition tells you.

4 Begin to sway and move gently to the rhythm, moving the focus of your energy into your belly area and feeling your feet in contact with the ground.

5 Ask your spirit helpers to show you your own special power dance. Continue to move to the rhythm and be patient. Let any new movements or steps develop; if they do not, experiment with any movements that feel pleasing.

6 Begin to make sounds to go with the movements. You might feel like using words that have a special meaning to you, repeating a short phrase about your own gifts or the way you connect with the Web of Life. Or you may simply make intuitive vowel sounds that give you a good feeling. The whole dance and song will probably not come to you at the first session.

7 Repeat the process until you have found your power song and dance.

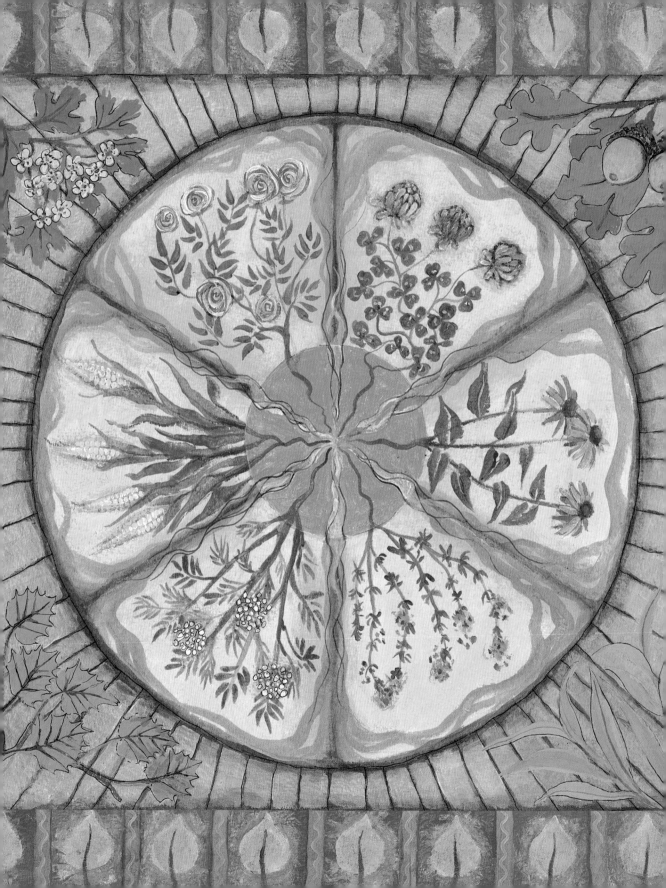

The plant people

Plants interact with humans in subtle ways, focusing and balancing our natural well-being. We experience this on an intuitive level whenever we are among plants, as we sense relaxation creeping over us or the lifting of our heart at a particular herb's scent or a flower's bright colours. Plants respond to different life situations as we do, and can even send signals over considerable distances to others of their own kind. As we begin to realize that plants are truly beings in their own right, we find that we are responding to their communications. A friend of mine, who had never 'felt' any connection to plants, began to hear her houseplants 'calling' to be watered as she developed her shamanic awareness.

We cannot pre-judge a plant's shamanic power by its appearance. In general, plants that are in their natural state – that is to say they have not been selectively bred by human intervention – have a clearer and stronger spirit energy. A plant that might be regarded as a common weed may be a powerful healing medicine or a plant spirit helper. Some shamans use the medicinal healing properties of a range of plants; others work with just one plant ally, or spirit helper, consulting it for answers to all the patient's needs.

Plants that alter states of consciousness – psychotropic plants, such as peyote and ayahuasco – can be used to induce trance in the shaman and sometimes in the patient, so that spirit help can be consulted. These are deeply respected as 'teacher' plants with very powerful spirit medicine, and they are gathered and used within strict ritual guidelines. To abuse their perception-altering gifts through social or recreational use is seen as an insult to the plant spirit, which may result in drastic 'lessons' for the user.

Getting in touch

Expand your awareness of plant medicine by making regular visits – perhaps a short daily walk – to greet a few plant people, trees or shrubs. Plants are always around, even in towns: eating into the bricks of old houses, pushing up through tarmac, shifting paving stones. Start by making a nodding acquaintance (as with the people you might meet in passing every day). Notice how they look, how their energy feels, whether they are in bud, are dropping leaves, where their roots are holding, whether they are in a sunny or shady situation. Greet them in different weathers and light conditions. Then, just as you notice how a person might change from day to day – looking happy or tired, wearing a sticking plaster or sporting a new haircut – you will see the plant people in their different moods and cycles of being.

Plant spirit medicines

Plant characteristics

Check out the following to get to know a plant's medicine qualities:

- Is the soil damp or dry?
- What is its height and spread?
- Is it in a clump or is it a single plant?
- Is it in a sunny or shady position?
- What is the shape of the leaf and vein pattern?
- What is the shape of the seeds or flowers?
- How do the stalks or branches divide?
- What are the pattern and colour of the stalk or trunk?
- What are its defence mechanisms (e.g., thorns)?
- What is its scent?
- What kind of presence does it have?

Traditional names usually refer to a plant's relationship with humans (for example, 'soapwort' has cleaning properties, while 'deadly nightshade' is very poisonous). If you note the plant's characteristics, it should be easy to look it up in one of the many excellent reference books now available.

Here are some common plants and trees, and a little bit about their individual spirit medicines.

Rose

Wild roses love hedgerows and sunny woodlands. If you watch a rosebud as it opens you clearly sense the medicine of this plant person. The tight spiral of petals packed inside the bud slowly unfurls, expanding from its heart and releasing a perfume that soothes and uplifts. But it is a well-defended beauty, being equipped with thorns to ensure gentle handling!

Rose energy is both powerful and gentle, with energizing, protecting and cleansing properties. It relates particularly to female sexuality and can be a powerful helper in recovering our sexual identity. It helps us restore our bonds with others and can help pregnant mothers to bond with their unborn children. As the perfume is exuded, it strengthens our spiritual awareness and compassion.

Clover

Clover can be found creeping among grass in the wild and in garden lawns. Children down the generations have searched for a 'lucky' four-leafed clover – a tradition that acknowledges this plant as a medicine that offers kindness, love and good luck. Clover is also said to be the favourite home of leprechauns. The heavy, sweet scent of its flowers is a favourite feeding ground for bees, and $2^{1}/_{2}$ acres (1 ha) of clover can yield up to 220 lb (100 kg) of delicious honey.

Its powerful root system demonstrates its persistent nature and reflects the need for us to hold on to our personal direction. Its roots do indeed enrich the soil they grow in, and clover has long helped people to strengthen their body's restorative and self-cleansing powers and speed recovery after illness.

Echinacea

There is a joyful sense of energy about this plant person, and it is a good ally to have when our body is under attack from a virus as it helps us muster our natural defences into a concerted effort of well-being, thus boosting the immune system.

Maize

Maize and its relatives in the corn family, connect us to the nurturing and physical aspects of Mother Earth. Maize has been widely used to symbolize fertility, abundance and Mother Earth's gifts. For the Hopi people of North America it is celebrated as the presence of Corn Woman, and in western Europe there are many ancient corn traditions centred on the Greek earth goddess, Demeter, and corn is still plaited into offerings or 'dolly' figurines at harvest-time.

When some grains of corn self-seeded in my urban backyard, I really discovered the power of this plant spirit. It brought a sense of grace and blessing to my garden.

Thyme

This low-growing, pungent herb grows wild on uplands, rocky outcrops and clifftops. Its strong, penetrating scent is readily released when the leaves are brushed. Thyme is used to purify sacred spaces and in healing rituals; it evokes and strengthens memory and links with the past. It can widen our psychic awareness and is valuable when exploring past issues and even past lives. Its cleansing medicine helps to fight infection, both internally and externally.

Grow some thyme around your doorway for protection and blessing. And place fresh sprigs around the home and workspace to keep away negativity.

Elder

'Elder Mother' grows as a shrub or small tree and is said to provide refuge for good fairies. If you brush against the foliage, it releases a pungent scent with a real sense of presence. In spring flat-topped bunches of creamy white blossom scent the air, later turning into clusters of glossy, dark red fruits that hang heavy with delicious juice.

Elderflower water can soothe coughs and colds, while the berry juice is a potent ally against viruses, cold symptoms and winter ailments. As new plants quickly grow from twigs pushed into the ground, its spirit medicine is linked to powers of rebirth, and elder is also known as the gatekeeper to the Otherworlds.

Harvest Ritual

Take some long stalks of corn or wild grass with seeds on. Plait the stalks together or bind them with decorative coloured threads. Hang them outside as a thanks offering for the abundance of Mother Earth and as a prayer for your own future needs.

Tree spirit medicine

T he tree members of the plant realm are capable of living to tremendous ages, with some species surviving for hundreds of years, remembering the seasons and climate changes within their annual rings. Trees provide shelter and succour to many relatives, including humankind. Tree spirits can form important relationships with many generations of shorter lived beings, and we can get to know both the medicine of a species and the personalities of individuals.

Willow Ritual

Find a straight willow twig and strip off its leaves and bark. Bind it into a circle with some thread and trim the ends. Leave the circle over an upturned plant pot overnight to dry. Decorate it with two threads or ribbons crossing in the centre and add beads, feathers or other decorations. Hang this Medicine Wheel symbol of balance and thanksgiving where you can see it often.

Willow

Willow sends its roots yards to find water and if you peel the bark from a tree, you will find that the wood beneath is wet and pliable. It is therefore closely associated with the Moon that influences the waters of Mother Earth. Willow has powerful regenerative powers: new growth springing up from fallen branches and tiny twigs stuck into the ground, even upside-down. This connects it with the unseen worlds and with our subconscious and immortality. Willow's powerful dreaming medicine can enhance visionary skills.

Through its affinity with water, willow also aids the release of deeply buried feelings via the flow of tears. Romany gypsies placed willow garlands on graves to help the soul move on to the spirit world and wore willow to show that they were grieving for a loved one.

Willow helps humans with illnesses associated with damp places, such as colds and rheumatism. A traditional bitter drink made from willow bark, containing the active ingredients of aspirin, lowered fevers and eased pain.

Oak Ritual

Gather acorns in the autumn and decorate your home with strings of them at the Winter Solstice to welcome back the Oak King or burn a Yule log of oak. Plant a few of the acorns in pots. They grow easily and will be gifts for friends and for the land later in the spring.

Oak

Steadfastness, strength and endurance are the medicine characteristics of oak. Oak trees can live to great ages and the wood itself actually strengthens with age, becoming as hard as iron. Oak trees provide homes for a wide variety of wildlife and on a summer's day you can hear the many different voices and wings above. As they tend to become hollow with age, there is often accommodation inside!

Of all the trees, oak is most often struck by lightning and so it is seen as a path of communication between Spirit and Creation. In Siberian mythology the Golden Oak connects heaven and earth; and the Druids use oak throughout the year in ceremony and ritual. At Midsummer in the northern hemisphere (21 June) a fire of oak is burned to show that the Oak King has been vanquished by the Holly King, who presides over the next half-year, until the Oak King returns once more at the Winter Solstice (22 December).

Hazel

Hazel is a small tree, which often grows from a many-stemmed base as new shoots have the power to grow directly from its roots. Its energy is robust, protective and sturdy. Its dancing yellow catkins are one of the first signs of spring, while hazel nuts are a highly nutritious and beneficial food source for humans, concentrating the tree's power and symbolizing the need to distil the essence of our knowledge and pass it on to future generations. Wisdom comes from this knowledge but must used with flexibility.

Staffs carried by pilgrims were made of hazel, as was Mercury's wand, the symbol of his healing wisdom. Dowsers have long used forked hazel twigs in their divining, watching for movement in them when crossing over underground water or sensing energy lines. Hazel's ability to impart knowledge has meant that in the past hazel twigs were even used to decide the guilt of thieves in the English judicial system.

Hazel wood is extremely pliable and can be split lengthwise and bent and twisted without breaking, making it widely used in fencing and house building. It makes ideal poles for the domes of 'benders', traditional Romany summer dwellings, and for the construction of the lodge in the 'sweat-lodge' ceremony (see page 67). The tree is associated with the element of air, and the air around a hazel is said to be charged with the power of inspiration.

Hazel Ritual

Make a protective talisman by cutting a slice through a section of hazel branch, drilling two holes near the centre and threading it on cord to wear around the neck or wrist or to tie to medicine items, such as rattles or drums.

Hawthorn

If you see a wind-battered tree clinging to an impossible crag, it is probably a hawthorn. Its tree medicine is one of toughness and resilience, and its gnarled trunk and roots withstand many tests. Hawthorn's vibrant energy in spring associates it with new life and new relationships, and branches were often carried at weddings to bless the marriage with children. Garlands were used in springtime rituals to bring blessing and good fortune, and leaves were scattered in cradles to protect newborn babies.

Clumps of hawthorn make wonderful sheltering and nesting places for small birds, which are able to feed on its vitamin-rich berries far into the winter.

Hawthorn has long, effective spikes, but these transform every year as they put forth new leaves and fragrant blossom. So hawthorn is a protector, but also a powerful ally for the heart, strengthening trust and forgiveness and bringing the heart into balance with itself. Beloved of the fairy folk, hawthorn is held sacred in many traditions, being the guardian to holy wells and springs and marking portals to other dimensions.

Hawthorn Ritual

If you are looking for a new beginning of some kind in your life, find a hawthorn tree and tie a piece of cotton thread or cloth to it (red is a good colour to use), telling the tree of your hopes and dreams and leaving a gift such as birdseed or water, or a bright glass bead, for the fairy folk.

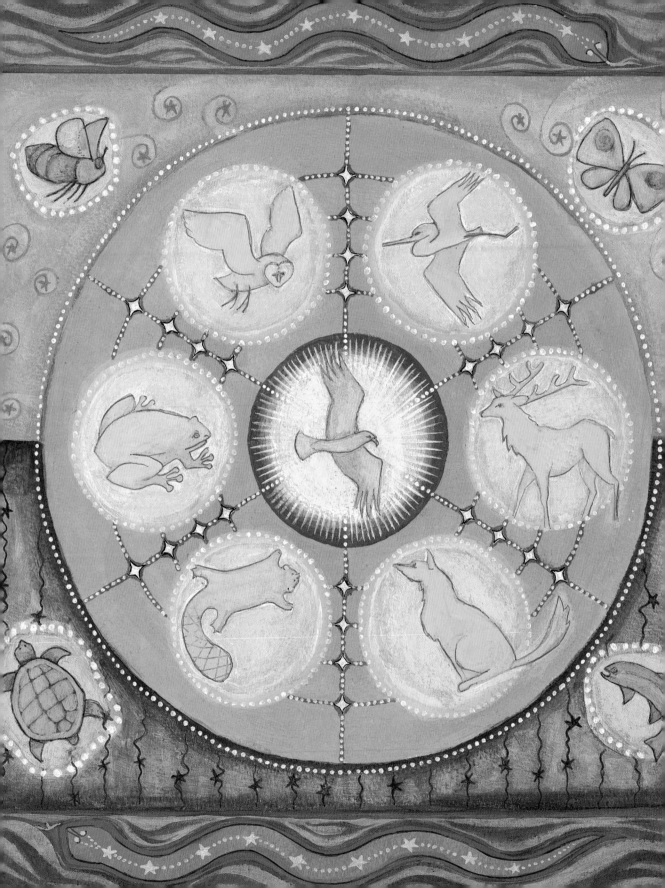

The animal powers

We cannot separate the details of a creature's lifestyle, its food sources and what preys on it from its spirit medicine. A mouse's jumping medicine helps it escape from the cat, while the changing medicine of a chameleon's skin gives it camouflage from predators. Each species has its own special way of fitting into the intricate Web of Life through its habitat and habits, diet and hunting skills, likes and dislikes. The medicine qualities may be easy to recognize in a dreaming bear or a roaring lion, but what of an earthworm or mosquito? On the Medicine Path there are no hierarchies of importance, and each creature's medicine power is an equally important thread in the weaving of the Web.

Animal watching

Nowadays there are many ways in which we can observe creatures: in wildlife parks, zoos and animal sanctuaries, as well as in the wild. Even in an urban landscape, if you know where and when to look, you can watch foxes and bats and the many species that live undetected in the heart of a city or on the verges of busy highways.

Feed birds on your windowsill or lawn and you will soon notice the different characteristics of their medicine: the brash aggression of starlings, the elegant determination of robins, and the amazing flying skills and tenacity of finches. Grow plants that attract insects, or go and see which plants attract bees and hoverflies in the park. If you have a river nearby, this offers a golden opportunity to sit and watch. Once you have developed your invisibility skills from the 'still hunt' (see page 30), you will notice so much more of what is going on in this crowded habitat.

Some people seem to attract certain creatures to them, without knowing how or why. These animals may have special medicine links with you and may indicate which animal spirits are already helping you. On a workshop I was running to help people find their animal spirit helpers, one of the participants was met on her shamanic journey by a fox, which readily agreed to be her spirit helper. Afterwards she shared with us that foxes had always 'visited' her: barking on her lawn and waking her in the middle of the night; even sitting in the middle of the road staring at her and causing her to stop her car. She really knew how to get what she wanted through quiet persistence and good stalking and certainly had the power to blend into the background when necessary.

Animal spirit medicine

Check out the following
to get to know an
animal's medicine
qualities:

- How can we detect its presence?
- What is its life cycle?
- What does it eat?
- What sounds does it make?
- Who are its natural predators?
- Where does it live?
- What particular skills does it show?
- How does it move?
- What speeds can it travel at?
- How do the seasons affect it?
- Does it migrate?

In myth and folklore the medicine powers of animals are clearly depicted: cunning fox, wise owl, trickster rabbit and coyote. These fabled qualities weave through the stories, echoing the attributes of the animals as they live in the everyday world. The following short profiles of animal medicine powers show how medicine reflects real life. Add to them from your own experience and observation, and make similar thumbnail sketches or 'medicine fact files' for yourself.

Bee

We watch bees drone past in summer, ever busy and always seemingly travelling with a sense of purpose. They travel far afield, exchanging news of good foraging grounds when they return to the hive, in the form of a dance. The dedication of the highly ordered bee community to the rearing of the next generation is legendary – guarding the hive with their lives, building intricate geometric nurseries and flying hundreds of miles to collect nectar to produce the life-giving honey for their young.

Bee medicine is that of duty and devotion to family, of bringing sweet blessings and fruitfulness, happiness and good fortune. Bees are therefore consulted on family matters, and a traditional bee keeper will always inform his hive of any major family or community events, especially births, marriages and deaths. Politeness and respect must be maintained in all dealings with bees.

Butterfly

When we admire a butterfly's colourful beauty we are seeing the final stage of a remarkable life cycle. This begins, of course, with a very different creature – a caterpillar that is completely focused on feeding and growing. When the caterpillar reaches its physical limit it shrouds itself in a cocoon, apparently dying and becoming inert. But within the cocoon the transformation continues until the butterfly emerges in a completely new form.

Butterfly medicine is about the cycles of life and the power that we each have to transform and re-create ourselves in a new form through one life or many. But if we witness the emergence of the butterfly from its cocoon, we see how difficult this process can be. Much energy goes into splitting the old skin and hauling the new form out, and even then the butterfly has to rest and inflate its wings after its rebirth. Any transformation takes effort and we must allow ourselves time to adjust to the new shape in which we may find ourselves. Ask for butterfly medicine to help you if you are seeking or undergoing change.

Spider

Often celebrated as the weaver and keeper of the Web of Life, the spider has a powerful female medicine and shows us the reality of the forces of creation and destruction as part of the natural cycle. The indomitable perseverance of a spider creating a web can only evoke our admiration. Yet that web has a purpose, and when insects get caught in it, we see the other side of the spider's power. For its lightning strike, its paralysing bite and its parcelling-up of the food to hang in its larder are efficient, precise and merciless.

Spiders make their homes in all kinds of living conditions: underground, high in trees, in any unswept corner of human habitation. They are devoted mothers, often carrying their young around on their backs to keep them safe.

Deer

The deer embodies prodigious stamina and athleticism. Its survival skills include the ability to run like the wind and jump high obstacles. Camouflage and stillness also form part of its defences – its young often being left alone in the open, hidden only by their dappled coats and their ability to lie unmoving in the shadows.

There is a deep gentleness at the heart of the deer's medicine power, which also gives it a reputation for a loving nature. The male is famously territorial over his herd of females and fearless in battle if his authority is challenged, while the autumn cries of rutting males are one of the great songs of the wild. So the deer holds a powerful medicine of tactics and patience in the face of danger, and determined and courageous love.

Wolf

The powerful, relentless lope of the wolf makes distances look easy, and the pack combines to bring down prey much larger than individual wolves by persistent teamwork and by wearing down their quarry to a state of exhaustion.

For wolves, the family is a disciplined unit within the pack: females have nursery rotas for their cubs, and eating is done in strict order of precedence. Wolf medicine is therefore about family, community order, discipline and leadership. A tracking wolf lifts its nose to the wind, reading the many scents it finds there. So the wolf also helps us find a trail and leads us along our spirit path, faithfully accompanying us as we search for our goals.

A Spider Blessing

Take two straight dried stems of sage or lavender a few inches long and of equal length. Tie them together at right angles (crossing at the centre) with a length of thread and continue to wind it clockwise passing once round each stem and keeping their crossed shape in place. Add on other coloured threads to make striped diamonds of colour until you have filled the stems.

Hang outdoors to celebrate the Web of Life.

Beaver

The glossy-coated beaver is the architect and shaper of the landscape. Two long, incurved front teeth can chisel around young trees and fell them in minutes to dam a river, creating the foundation of the substantial 'lodges' in which they live. Lodges can be occupied by many generations of beavers, which live in comfortable chambers inside, snug and safe above the water line.

The whole surrounding area is managed by the beavers, with streams maintained to keep up the supply of water to the pond formed by the dam, with the beavers maintaining water levels by means of twig-and-branch sluices woven into it. A beaver's medicine power designs and builds, regulates energy and organizes good protection and shelter for the family.

Turtle Therapy

If you are feeling world-weary or vulnerable why not ask turtle medicine to give you a bit of nurturing. Take a blanket and smudge it and yourself, then find a quiet undisturbed place to sit with the blanket around you as a 'shell'. Tuck your head and extremities into it as much as you need and feel the comfort of Mother Earth around you, protecting and covering you like the blanket.

Turtle

This ancient relative's body is armoured with bony platelets, covered with a solid shell above and below, into which it can withdraw its limbs and head to escape predators or patiently sit out an attack. The turtle teaches us the lessons of being protected and having a shell to retreat into when we need it

Not only does the turtle's line of ancestry reach back more than 200 million years, but individuals can live well into their second century. Recognizing this ancient lineage, Native North Americans call their land Turtle Island, in honour of the first turtle on whose back the land was created. Turtle medicine is closely allied to the energies of Mother Earth, and the turtle shows us how to be grounded and focus on the practical issues in life. Turtle medicine moves slowly, but gets where it needs to go – a valuable lesson to most of us!

Salmon

This renowned navigator retraces its path across whole oceans to return to its birthplace and spawn the next generation. The salmon finds its home river estuary and journeys uphill over many natural obstacles – up weirs and waterfalls – leaping again and again until it finds the pool in which it was hatched. This prodigious feat gives salmon its reputation as a keeper of wisdom and the knowledge of ancestral lineage.

We all know how difficult it is to travel against our own particular currents in life, but we can take strength from the salmon's courage, dedication and perseverance. Salmon medicine also teaches us trust of the instinct that guides us to our own heart and truth.

Owl

The haunting cry of an owl in the hours of darkness reveals its medicine as the messenger of dreams. The owl is a master of silent watching, its head able to swivel without moving the rest of its body, its distinctive flat face giving it clear forward vision. An owl's feather is soundproofed by a delicate additional fringing that goes all round the edge of the feather, silencing the flow of air over its surface. Add to this a body that is stocky and knife-sharp talons, and you have an efficient hunter.

If you meet an owl's silent gaze you may feel that it is penetrating your inner senses, seeking what is hidden. The owl sees what lies there and calls it forth. Its spirit medicine has long had the reputation for clear-sighted wisdom and for delivering justice; the owl calls us to develop our intuitive abilities to see through self-deceit and reach our own place of knowing.

Eagle

The eagle flies so high that it seems to disappear from this reality. From these great heights, as it hangs motionless on the thermals, it can see its quarry in detail on the ground and drops like a stone to the kill. As the eagle lives in this daily connection between the earth and the far reaches of the sky, it helps us to remain in touch with our spirit self. The eagle is asked to be our messenger to the unseen realms.

The eagle's power of vision and ability to see the 'big picture' while targeting specific goals, reveals its medicine gift of vision-in-action. Eagle feathers are much prized in many cultures, especially among the Plains people of North America, where they are awarded as symbols of personal strength, courage, wisdom and living true to one's own personal vision.

Heron

A heron has an easy elegance and a slow, sweeping flight, its long neck folded along its back, its legs trailing gracefully. The males have a stately courtship dance, and pairs return to the same large, untidy nest year after year. The heron's long legs are built for wading through the edges of pools and rivers or for standing patiently in shallow water, waiting for its quarry to swim by before it strikes.

Their spirit medicine is about the keeping of secrets, the holding of hidden knowledge and the ability to look deeply within. The heron's reputation for being the first bird to greet the dawn links it to the coming of new life, and it is said to bring the gift of fertility and to guide new souls to their birth incarnation.

Feather Prayer

A feather can be stuck into the earth as a simple way of asking for a blessing for all our relations, or for a specific prayer or request you may have in your heart. Alternatively, look through the feather at a candle flame and make your prayer to the rainbow that you will find there.

Stone spirit medicine

The stone people have many forms: they may live in the massive shape of mountains, forming the bones of Mother Earth, or be as fine as the drifting sands of the desert.

The kind of stone that lies beneath a landscape influences which plants grow there, the way water flows over and through it and the creatures that dwell there. Bare granite may be dramatically visible in outcrops and cliffs, while soft layers of chalk may underpin a grassy downland. There are many variations – find out what the geological map of your own environment is like and visit other kinds of landscape to feel the difference. Look at the lie of the land; sense through your feet and touch with your hands to get a 'feel' of the bones beneath the landscape. Seams of quartz crystal, for instance, may affect your sense of focus, and large deposits of it can make some people feel disorientated.

Stone-people lodge

This ancient ceremony has taken many different forms throughout the world and throughout time. Sometimes called the 'sweat lodge' or 'purification lodge', it is a sacred process of cleansing on all levels and can bring about powerful change, healing and vision.

A low, dome-like structure of bent saplings is covered with blankets to make it light- and airproof, leaving a small doorway just large enough to crawl through. A small pit is dug inside this lodge, and a sacred fire is lit outside in line with the door and fire pit. A fire spirit energy line now connects all three parts. Stones are heated in the fire until they glow with the heat they are holding. The ceremony participants then go into the lodge, symbolically entering Mother Earth's womb of darkness, potential and the unknown. When all are seated inside, the hot rocks are welcomed into the lodge, placed in the fire pit and sprinkled with water and herbs, filling the tiny space with clouds of aromatic steam. The ceremony proceeds with prayers, chanting and periods of silence, and the leader may use his healing skills on one or more of those present. After being in a stone-people lodge one is left with a deep feeling of well-being, connection to the Web and the inner stillness of the stone people, which may last for some days.

The leader of a sweat-lodge should be well trained and experienced, respectful of the limitations and wishes of the participants, and able to work with the way elemental and other spirit energies may behave within a sacred space. There are certain contra-indications for entering a sweat-lodge, such as medical or mental health conditions, and advice should be sought from a medical practitioner beforehand.

Building awareness

Another way to develop a sense of the great variety of stone people is to cultivate the habit of collecting stones. As you build up your collection, don't look for particularly exotic or 'special' stones; just let them call to you as they did on your Blessing Stones Trail (see page 33). When you get them home, wash them, thank them for visiting you and put them in a bowl or basket where you will see them often.

Get into the habit of picking up one or two stones, feeling their weight and texture, their warmth or coldness, their marks and their shape from different angles – simply getting to know them. You will soon begin to distinguish stones of different qualities, sensing their individual medicines. We must always be ready to return them to their natural environment if we receive the thought or impulse to do so, respecting that they are living relatives and not simply dead bits of the earth.

There is an ancient tale of a Chinese emperor who sent his son to a venerable sage to learn how to identify true jade. For a year the old one placed a green stone in the youth's hand and told him all kinds of stories and tales. At the end of this time, weary with not being instructed in how to identify jade, the youth challenged him: 'No more stories; today you will do as my father commanded and start to tell me how to identify true jade!' The sage shrugged and placed a green stone in the youth's hand once more but, before he could say anything, the emperor's son cried out: 'Hey, what trick is this – this is not jade …'

This is how shamanic awareness works: by a deep sense of, and connection to, the essence of what is around us. Of course, during that year the youth had held true jade and had absorbed an awareness of it, using body- and not mind-knowledge.

Special stone helpers

In many tribal traditions it is usual to have a particular stone companion that you can consult. It is not generally a crystal or gem, as these have very particular energy vibrations and help us in quite specific ways (some of which are described opposite). Traditionally these stone helpers, called 'wotai' by the Lakota Sioux, are kept in pouches and are cleaned and smudged regularly.

If you find such a stone and wish to ask it for guidance, explain the situation you are trying to deal with. Let your inner sense converse with the stone and try not to be analytical about what goes on, but let the stone person's 'replies' come to you through your own thoughts and sensations. And, just like any friend, sometimes they are available and sometimes not.

Gems and crystals

Stones with specific kinds of energy can bring balance and change into our life. They may also be fixed to ceremonial objects, such as rattles and drums, or worn for their special qualities. Here are descriptions of a few of these stone people and their medicines.

Agate

This smooth, hard stone has bands of different colours, some of which may be almost transparent. It is a powerful healer with a grounding effect. It promotes confidence in the future and when facing change or discrimination. It is especially effective for practical and material concerns. Moss agate, a variety with tiny tree-like patterns, is especially helpful in connecting us with the plant realm.

Clear quartz

This stone, which has a good general healing energy, can be found in perfect multi-faceted, pointed crystal forms. It is a good crystal for beginners to work with and can be programmed to help you in specific ways. Clear quartz stimulates mental clarity and focus.

Rose quartz

Rose quartz is rarely found in crystal form. It has a gentle pink colouration with soft translucent qualities, but this colouring can fade if the stone is subjected to heat, for example if it is left on a sunny window sill. The affirming qualities of rose quartz are used when we wish to promote positive dreaming and it can be used to enhance our creativity. It also relates to the heart and issues of trust and can help ease feelings of anger, fear, guilt, jealousy and other strong emotions.

Jade

This green stone is very hard and does not split easily, and it was therefore used in ancient times for making weapons and tools. Jade promotes positive attitudes to life and protects and strengthens the life force. In China, where it is highly prized, it is said to increase longevity, strengthen the physical body and make men more fertile. It has a nurturing and peaceful quality, promoting emotional balance.

Jasper

A hard, smooth stone that varies in colour from pale yellow to deep blood-red, jasper helps with problems of the bladder and kidneys. It is used to aid tissue renewal and to promote physical and emotional grounding. It can also be used to treat nightmares and disturbed dream states.

Turquoise

The gentle blues and greens of turquoise can be laced with veins of silver, with which it is a perfect partner. Revered as a sacred and ceremonial stone across the world, turquoise is widely used for protection on all levels (seen and unseen) and for empowering and balancing. It relates especially to the throat area and strengthens clear communication, while holding a calming, peaceful quality. Turquoise is often left as a heartgift to Mother Earth after prayer or ceremony.

CHAPTER FOUR
Soul Health

Connecting with the energies around us

We each have an energy body that extends beyond our physical skin surface. This bubble of personal energy is often referred to as the 'aura'. Normally the aura cushions us from the stresses of life, but if we are under physical or emotional stress, this protection may be weakened and we may feel that life is penetrating our normal defences.

The aura is permeable, just like our physical skin, and can develop holes if we are shocked, injured, sick or afraid. Our vital energy can then leak out through the breach, and other external energies may filter in. Protection varies from individual to individual; for instance, one person may not be bothered by a colleague shouting angrily, but this anger energy may penetrate the auric field of another person, leaving them feeling vulnerable, pinned down or exhausted.

If you feel that a situation or person is, literally, getting under your skin, remember the circumstance so that you can prepare yourself to be better protected next time you meet it. This can be done quite simply by exercising aura awareness and practising keeping it 'closed'. Then, when you meet that challenging situation again, it will be second nature to make sure that your aura remains intact and doing its job.

Strengthening the aura is very simple but takes a little practice. Thought has the power to control it, and we can use mind power to imagine a protective layer of some kind around our body. This 'magic skin' can be anything that you can immediately call to mind. Look at the list and see which images appeal to you, then experiment with them. Nothing should go in or out of this layer without your knowledge and agreement. So any negativity that may have crept in can be ejected from your system using your intent, with the aura surface acting like a one-way membrane.

People often ask if strengthening their aura might close them off from fully experiencing life or make them less loving. In fact, the opposite is true. The more we feel secure and in charge of our own energy field, the more we can be at ease in our life situations and respond with compassion and confidence. As you explore shamanic awareness you are meeting new situations, so it is important to be aware of your personal energy levels and the condition of your auric defences. Regular smudging (see page 15) will help keep your aura, and the spaces in which you operate, protected and clean.

Magic skins

The best image for you to use as a magic skin is the one you find easiest. Imagining a dustbin liner around yourself is just as effective as an exotic blue cloak, as long as your body is completely covered, with no gaps. Be honest about what works best for you. Remember – no one else can see it! Here are a few suggestions:

- A space suit
- An egg shell
- A colour: blue, gold and red are all traditionally favoured
- A sound, such as sleigh bells, drum beats or wind song
- A scent, such as sage or cedar
- White or coloured light.

Energy from earth and sky

No matter how well we maintain our aura, we all need to replenish our energy supplies at times. The energy renewal exercise that follows is described as taking place outdoors, but once you are used to it you can do it at any time when your energy feels depleted: in a traffic jam, before a business meeting or family celebration, at the dentist's or at a party. By practising it beforehand, in a more tranquil setting, you will be able to keep your focus and renew your energy when the conditions are less than ideal.

Energy renewal

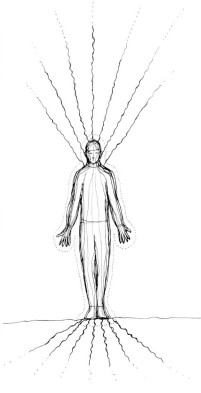

1 Find a place in nature where you will be undisturbed and preferably alone.

2 Stand with your head upright, as if a thread were connected to your crown and were pulling it gently up towards the sky. Keep your feet firmly planted on the ground.

3 Call to mind your aura and make sure that your magic skin is in place. Keep checking throughout the exercise that it remains intact. Breathe quietly and naturally.

4 Now focus on Mother Earth beneath you and feel how she supports your weight. In your imagination ask her beneficial energy to flow into you. Feel it rise gently up through your feet and legs until it fills all of you. You may experience the energy as having a colour, sound or sensation, or you may feel nothing in particular. Your experience may vary whenever you repeat the exercise, or it may remain constant.

5 When you feel filled with energy from Mother Earth, turn your attention to the expanse of sky above you. You cannot touch Father Sky, and yet he is always there. Invite his beneficial energy to come down through your crown and shoulders, until it fills all of you.

6 When you feel that this is complete, thank your sacred parents for their help, in whatever way feels right for you.

Shamanic tools

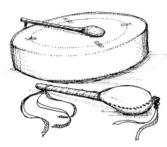

The drum and rattle are worldwide shamanic tools that can be used simply and effectively to help shift awareness into a state of conscious trance. Shamans have used them for countless ages, and there are many historical images depicting their use in shamanic ritual on cave walls, drums and ceremonial clothing.

Shamanic drums come in many forms and sizes, but the most common is the round 'frame' drum, where animal skin is stretched over one side of a wooden hoop, with a handle at the back to hold it by. Each culture has its own style, and the shaman is often instructed by spirit helpers in how to make, decorate and play his or her own drum. Such drums are personal to the shaman, and other people are not permitted to play them.

The drum is played during sacred dances, songs and healing processes. The usual rhythm is a rapid, monotonous 200–280 beats a minute (roughly the equivalent of theta brainwaves). This shifts brain activity into dream-state patterns and helps the shaman connect to the spirit worlds. The drum beat, sometimes called the 'shaman's horse', carries the shaman on his journeys into the spirit realms and brings him safely back along the return trail to everyday reality.

Rattles, which are used in similar ways to drums, have a higher vibrational effect, being especially useful in breaking up and dispersing heavy, stagnant energies – just think how much babies appreciate this in their static early world. Rattles can also detect energy blockages in people and places. If you have a rattle (you can improvise with a plastic tub filled with rice), try walking around a room shaking it gently with the intention of harmonizing the energies, letting the rattle guide you. Relax into it and don't let the mind dictate your actions. You will find that your rattle lingers in certain areas, especially in corners where the energy gets sluggish, and may vary in speed and even sound quality. You can use rattles in this way to cleanse, as an effective alternative to smudging.

Contemporary shamanic practitioners often live in circumstances where loud drumming or even rattling is difficult. One answer is to use a drumming tape played through headphones. This is not as far removed from live drumming as it seems: after all, it is the rhythm of the drumming or rattling that is key to shifting the consciousness. Try drumming or rattling to a slow 'heartbeat' rhythm while sitting in your power place (see page 50), and feel its relaxing after-effect. When you are more used to it, try doing this before entering the silence (see page 19) and again immediately after you return, to ground you.

Ceremonial rattles and drums

These rattles and drums sometimes have specific jobs to do, and they are usually kept wrapped up and out of sight until they are needed. Like all ceremonial objects, they can become charged with the intent and energy of their purpose. This is no different from the energy that we may sense in an old violin or a religious icon. Much-used shamanic tools can disorientate people and environments if they are not handled with respect, because of their role in shifting energies.

Visiting the helpers

Once you have established links with your own helpers (see following pages) you can visit them at your outdoor power place (see page 50) to ask them questions and to receive advice and help with your own balancing and healing processes. Keep these meetings within this familiar territory and explain to them that you cannot venture beyond it without more specialized and specific training in shamanic journeying. It is often more practical to access this outdoor power place from your indoor one (see page 51) where you will be undisturbed and can concentrate your attention fully. If indoors, establish a firm sense of your outdoor power place within your inner eye before you begin. If outside, enter the silence (see page 19) to stretch your shamanic awareness and prepare yourself. When you feel ready, call to the helpers you know and state your question four times. If they do not appear make a still hunt (see page 30) reflecting on your question.

Having a reason to visit

Visiting the spirit helpers is always done with a clear, specific intention and time limit, which must be decided before you begin. This means that you know *why* you are visiting your helpers, and so do they. The spirits can then deliver their responses more clearly and you will be better able to interpret them, for their replies are linked *specifically* to the question or request for help that you have made.

Your original intention must be remembered at all times during the visit and when reflecting on your experiences afterwards. Often the spirits respond to your question through the 'story' that unfolds during your visit, in which you play a key part. Or they may respond by giving you gifts of power or healing: you may be offered special food to eat, may be washed in light or grow wings – there are countless beautiful ways and every visit is unique. After all, this gateway has been created through the action of your own intention within sacred space, and the 'normal' structures of time and space do not apply. So be prepared for the landscape to shift and change in a dream-like way as the story unfolds.

You always stay in charge of this experience and can refuse anything that you feel unhappy with. You take decisions just as you do in the everyday world and can even choose to return before your intended time limit if you wish. As long as you thank your allies and any other spirit helpers, and behave respectfully as a visitor should, the spirit helpers will understand.

Further steps

Full shamanic journeying trance is not always suitable for everyone to practise; it needs individual guidance to start with and instruction in certain safety measures. If you wish to take your trance experience further you need to seek guidance from a trained shamanic practitioner.

Plant spirit helpers

The shaman gains knowledge in the same way as the scientist, through observation and personal experience. A shaman may describe a plant such as yarrow as a 'herb for the wounded' and use it alongside ritual, songs and dances. The chemist, however, will define it as containing tannin and alkaloids, while the medical herbalist will prescribe it for its fever-reducing and antiseptic properties. All this information is true and valuable.

The shamanic approach is to connect with the living essence – the *spirit medicine* that the plant holds – and to treat the plant as a person, a fellow-relative in Creation. This connection is easiest with wild plants, because they have stronger and clearer energy voices.

Meeting a plant person

1 To make your own shamanic investigation of plant spirit medicine, find a place in nature and call to meet a plant that will help you. Try not to guess what it will be like. Relax and let your shamanic senses guide you.

2 Once you have found a plant to connect with, sit or stand by it. If this is impracticable, ask the plant's permission to take a small piece of leaf home with you and continue the process in your indoor power place. This fragment will hold the same essential qualities as the whole plant, but treat this gift of its body with respect; offer it back to Mother Earth with a prayer of thanks when you have finished.

3 Come to the South of the plant – the place of the emotions.* Greet the plant and ask how it is feeling today. What do you sense? Be aware of your own feelings as you make heart contact.

4 Move to the West of the plant – the place of physicality. Touch it gently, connecting through your physical senses and experiencing its textures, scent, sound and colours.

5 Move to the North of the plant – the place of the mind. Gather all the facts you can: has it any flowers or seeds, is it in light or shade, wet ground or dry?

6 Move round to sit or stand at the East of the plant – the place of the spirit. Unfocus your eyes and let your inner senses receive any non-physical information about the plant's medicine power.

7 Return to sit at the South of the plant. Thank it for its help, and leave a heartgift (see pages 30–31).

* If you do not have a compass, guess the direction of South by the position of the sun in the sky, or designate South with your intention, keeping the same relative positions for the other directions. This is known as using the Magical Directions.

A special medicine relationship

Do you have a deep love of a certain flower or of the scent of a particular herb? Why does your heart gladden at the sight of one tree rather than another? Within the plant realm we all have special relationships that are like long-lasting friendships. Such plant spirits have probably been communicating with you for quite a while – perhaps for all your life. Knowing a plant ally is a two-way relationship, and the plant spirit will also benefit from contact with human spirit energy.

Finding your plant ally

You will need: smudge-kit (see page 15); a selection of stones, flowers or other natural objects; a bowl of water.

1 Go to either your outdoor or indoor power place.

2 Set up a sacred space using smudge and calling in the Four Directions.

3 Mark a circle about 3 ft (1 m) across, using stones, flowers or whatever feels right to you.

4 Make an offering of water to the circle and say:
'I am [state your name] and I call in a sacred manner to meet a plant that will be a beneficial ally for my earthwalk at this time.'

5 Sit at the East of the circle, focusing on the space within it as if it were a blank screen or empty stage. Relax and allow your shamanic awareness to expand, taking in everything that is happening without interpretation or judgement. You may experience a scent, a colour or a sensation in your own energy field. The name or image of the plant may suddenly appear in the circle or enter your mind.

6 As soon as you have a strong impression of a plant presence, thank it and ask if it has any message or gift for you at this time and if there is anything you can give it in return. Ask if there is anything it wishes to tell you now about its spirit medicine.

Safety notes – Plants affect our physical and mental systems if taken internally; some have powerful spirit medicines that can cause serious illness and even death. *Do not take any plant medicine internally without the advice of an experienced practitioner.*

Developing the relationship

- Keep seeds or pieces of your plant ally in a small pouch in your power place or round your neck so that it hangs close to your heart.
- Find pictures of the plant; or, even better, make diagrams, drawings or take photographs of it yourself.
- Wear the colours and/or scent from your plant.
- Ask your plant for a song that you can sing about its medicine.
- Dance the medicine of your plant as you did in the tree dance (see page 27).
- Grow the plant in your own garden or visit it in its natural habitat.
- Find facts about its everyday form, its cultivation needs and place of origin.
- Explore any known healing and traditional uses.

Animal spirit helpers

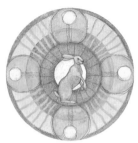

The term 'animal' is used to cover all members of the creature realm, from earthworms to eagles, from jellyfish to tigers. In the spirit worlds the animals are able to communicate with us through speech or mind-to-mind. However, they are quick to correct anyone who shows attitudes that are anthropomorphic (attributing human form or behaviour to animals) or patronizing. A spirit wolf once made it very clear to me that he did *not* fetch sticks! But spirit animals also have a deep warmth and playfulness when we respect them.

Before you seek your own animal ally, try communicating with the animal spirits to learn about their individual medicines. They have both species characteristics and personal traits, just as humans do. Follow the process below to meet at least four animals. It is often easier to develop sensing skills through comparative experiences; working with several animals contrasts the differences between them and helps you notice specific medicine qualities.

Connecting with the creatures

You will need: a selection of animal items; a clean mat or cloth; smudge-kit (see page 15).

1 Decide which four animals' medicine you would like to find out more about. Then choose something to represent each animal: a photograph, fur, a bone or feather, or its name written on a card. (Deciding whether to use animal parts for shamanic practice is something everyone must resolve for themselves. If the parts are used with respect, then the spirits seem to have no problem with this; indeed, shamans are often instructed by their spirit helpers to use teeth, claws, bones, fur or feathers in their work.)

2 Sit quietly and comfortably in a place where you will not be disturbed. Lay the animal items on the ground in front of you on your mat or cloth. Smudge yourself, the surrounding area and the animal items. Call in the Four Directions.

3 Bring your attention to the first animal item and pick it up. Explain that you are a two-legged relative and would like to know more about its medicine qualities. Explore it in detail with all your senses: look at its colour, shape and markings; smell it; feel its texture. If you are working with an image or word, imagine that you are doing this with the real creature. Ask it questions about its habitat, its likes and dislikes, its fears and delights. Do not interpret or edit out anything that doesn't fit with what you already know.

4 Ask the animal if there is anything else you need to be shown at this time.

5 Thank the animal and return the item to the mat. Take up the next item and repeat the process until you have made a connection with all four animals. When you have finished, thank the animals and smudge to close the process.

Finding your animal ally

You will need: smudge-kit (see page 15) or a candle; drum or rattle (optional).

1 Choose a time when you will have at least thirty minutes free of interruptions and go to your indoor power place. Smudge or light a candle – do whatever feels right to make the space active. If you have a drum or rattle, you might like to sound this on a steady beat for a couple of minutes to still your mind.

2 Sit with a straight spine or lie down; feel comfortable and relax. Take a few minutes to connect within yourself with your outdoor power place. When you feel ready, state your intention out loud *four* times:

'I wish to meet an animal helper that will be my ally at this time.'

3 Look all round your outdoor power place and note the kinds of leaves, grasses and stones that are there. What is the weather like and what time of day is it? What can you hear and smell? Expand your shamanic senses to become aware of all that happens. You may notice a shift of light, a change in the weather, new sounds, details about the landscape that had previously escaped you, or even tracks or spoor indicating your animal's presence. Your animal helper may appear at once or you may have to wait a while. Do not wait passively. Imagine yourself walking around the immediate area, but do not wander too far; look up, down, under, round, and keep making your request. Notice *everything*.

4 Once you see an animal clearly, ask if it is your ally. If the answer is unclear or a definite no, ask if it can help you find your ally or if it has a message for you.

5 When you feel that the visit is over, thank your helper and explain that it is time for you to leave. Let the experience of the power place gently dissolve, and return your awareness to everyday reality. Make a note of all that has happened and check that you have fully returned with some grounding exercises (see page 47).

6 If you do not meet your animal ally on the first visit, keep trying. Everyone has a helper of this kind, and the most usual barrier to meeting it is that the mind tries to 'help' and confuses the experience. You will soon sense when this is happening. Return your focus by going back to the original starting point and restating your intent.

Strengthening the ties

Make your links with your animal helper stronger by:

- Wearing amulets or jewellery depicting the animal
- Having pictures and photographs of the animal around your home and workplace
- Dancing the animal's medicine dance
- Giving practical support to the animal in ordinary reality through wildlife or conservation programmes
- Finding videos or sound recordings of your animal
- Collecting items associated with your animal and putting them in a small medicine pouch to wear or keep where you can see it regularly.

Establishing a daily ritual

- Keep a candle dedicated to peace and balance. Light it each morning, watch the flame and connect with Father Sky and Mother Earth. Blow it out, sending a blessing for the day ahead.
- Smudge yourself and offer smoke to each Direction in turn, asking their powers to be with you through the day.
- Sing your power song as an offering of your own presence in life and to charge up your energy batteries.
- Make sure that your 'magic skin' is intact, reinforcing it if necessary. Ask Spirit's blessing and protection for the day ahead.
- Greet your spirit helpers or guardian angels and ask them to be with you. Offer them smudge or take a moment to dance or sing with them.
- Drum or rattle quietly for a few moments to centre and still yourself and to connect with the rhythms of the earth and sky and the wonderful Web of Life.

Keeping in touch every day

Many of us live in communities that have few sacred links left with the Web of Life. In this sacred vacuum it is easy to lose touch with the shamanic perspective. A daily 'connection' ritual is a simple, quick and effective way to keep in touch.

The daily ritual is best done in the morning, before too many distractions set in and to give you a sense of connection with which to start the day. But it has to be practical and fit in with your commitments. It is *your* ritual and should be something that you look forward to each day. It should blend easily with your lifestyle – it really is possible for *everyone* to find a sacred slot for this important recharging and renewing activity. Remember that whatever each of us does affects the whole of Creation, so it brings blessings not only on you but on all whom you touch within the Web.

I have offered some suggestions here, and within the other exercises and sacred processes of this book you will find further inspiration. If the first form of ritual that you choose isn't working for you, don't give up: identify what the problem is. For instance, the process may be too elaborate, take too long, be done at the wrong time of day or not be 'portable' enough if you move around a lot. Once you have thought about it, adapt the original – or try something completely different that is more practical for you, and maybe more fun!

Everyday places of connection

A daily ritual often takes place at a personal altar, where the items needed for it can be kept to hand and where the room is familiar with sacred activity. You may already have a few precious medicine items such as crystals, animal carvings or divination cards, and these can be displayed on your personal altar space or on a small table or shelf that is kept regularly cleansed and dusted. Alternatively you may want to keep them in more portable form in a box, or wrapped in a beautiful cloth, which can also be used for laying them out whenever they are unwrapped. This is most conveniently kept in your indoor power place or sanctuary.

We instinctively make shrines to express and reflect what is important to us, whether this is the collection of family photos on the mantelpiece, a hanging Medicine Wheel symbol, a Buddhist statue or the pebbles we collected on a special beach that grace the windowsill. We may not give these special places a label, but they are natural expressions in outer reality of our inner world. We often have an instinctive gut feeling as to what should be included.

An altar or shrine is made with *sacred* intent, and this makes it slightly different. It then becomes a connecting place that is tuned in to a certain spiritual energy or purpose. We may, for instance, create an altar to bring peace and harmony into our home and to those who visit it. This could be placed in a hallway or on the doorstep. We may create an altar to connect with the Web of Life, and gather statues and carvings of our favourite creatures, plants, crystals and pebbles, like a garden of celebration.

The more focused the sacred intent behind an altar, and the more it is used, the more we sense its power as a spiritual gateway, a place where we can come to make contact with a particular aspect of Spirit. We can feel this power at shrines and altars in temples, churches and healing sanctuaries. This may not always feel comfortable, depending on our history, experience and ability to stay grounded.

The arrangement of objects on an altar is done thoughtfully, with a sense of sacred play, moving things around until they 'feel' right and a sacred harmony or wholeness has been established. If we allow an altar to become untidy or dusty, we may experience some confusion in our own energy. A cloth should always be spread over the area where the altar is laid out. This designates the sacred boundaries of the altar. If we wish to have an altar 'sleep' or become inactive, a cloth can simply be placed over it.

A personal medicine altar

We are each unique individuals with our own gifts and challenges, learning how to become fully who we are. No two babies (even twins) are alike, just as no two leaves on a tree are the same. This is how life continually re-creates itself – and who are we to argue? Strange, then, that we are rarely encouraged to reflect on this unique shape, to discover who we are and to celebrate it.

Personal medicine is that subtle mixture of traits and desires, abilities and fears, limitations and aptitudes of which we are made. It is a sacred collection of gifts, through which we connect with ourselves and the world. Not all those gifts are necessarily comfortable: anger may be one of them, or intense passion.

A personal medicine altar is a collection of objects that represents who we are, what is important to us and what issues we are working with. The items will change over time, and it becomes apparent when something no longer feels connected with the altar. Other items may show that they want to be added. While some key items generally remain throughout, much of the altar's content is a shifting landscape, reflecting our own processes of change. Such an altar is personal, and it may be that other people are not permitted to touch it. There are no correct aesthetics to this kind of medicine altar: traditional shamans' altars include anything from eagle feathers to plastic statues of saints; from perfume to herbs; from animal carvings to photographs of honoured teachers or power places. The Flowering Tree Ceremony (see opposite) will give you more valuable information about your medicine self and, using that information, you may like to start assembling your own personal medicine altar.

There are some rituals that are used again and again, providing valuable guidance and support. The Flowering Tree Ceremony (see opposite) is one of these. 'Flowering Tree' refers to the sacred tree at the centre of the world in the Native American Plains tradition – the Tree of Life.

Finding your personal medicine

As you come to ask a question to the Tree of Life in the following ceremony you look outwards at each of the Four Directions to watch for their reply. In this way you 'read' the response of the Web from within your sacred ceremonial space. An actual tree is normally used to stand for the Tree of Life, but if this is not possible you can use a representational tree such as a marker twig or seed cone.

Any questions can be asked during this ceremony, but the most relevant question in your quest to explore your personal medicine is 'Who am I?' Note everything that you experience, and not just the things you might regard as significant. Make a note of what you observe, either at each Direction or after all four have been completed. If you are writing down notes, keep them brief so that you can maintain your focus: a few key words will help you remember, and you can write up your description more fully afterwards.

A personal medicine pouch

A collection of small items that reflect your personal medicine can be placed in a pouch worn around your neck or tied to a belt. This miniature 'altar' helps you to remember your sacred selfhood and can be strenghtening in difficult situations.

Flowering Tree Ceremony

You will need: a heartgift; a tree (actual or representational); smudge-kit (see page 15).

1 Select a tree that is willing to work with you.

2 Smudge around the base of the tree, going clockwise around it. Then smudge yourself.

3 Starting at the South and travelling clockwise, walk around the tree to face each Direction and ask for its help and blessing.

4 Go to the South of the Flowering Tree and stand or sit close to it, with your back to the trunk. Ask your question: 'Who am I?' Watch everything to the South, observing closely and noting all that happens.

5 Go to the West of the Flowering Tree and ask as before, watching this Direction.

6 Go to the North of the Flowering Tree and ask as before, watching this Direction.

7 Go to the East of the Flowering Tree and ask as before, watching this Direction.

8 Return to the South, thank the Flowering Tree and leave your heartgift (see page 31).

9 Complete and close the sacred space in a way that is appropriate and right for you. Make sure you are grounded and fully back in everyday reality.

Asking Spirit questions

We can speak to Spirit about anything, and we are received without judgement or prejudice and with unconditional love. No special knowledge, intermediary or language is necessary – all we need do is speak with respect, from our hearts, as honestly as we can.

But there are times when we need to consult spirit allies and teachers or to look for reflections from the Four Directions of the Medicine Wheel. At these times we need to frame our requests and questions in ways that are very clear and concise. We are seeking a direct response, and if the question is simple and clear, this enables us to interpret the reply more accurately. If we ask broad questions, we will receive very general replies, which are often hard to make sense of. We therefore need to be specific; this also helps us to clarify exactly what it is we are asking for ourselves.

Avoid questions that have a yes/no answer, such as 'Will I pass this exam?' It would be more helpful to ask 'How can I improve my memory?' or 'Why am I so afraid of failure?' You can even ask your spirit allies to give you appropriate energy by saying, 'Could I have an energy gift that will help me in my exam?'

By learning to identify the important questions that we need to ask, we take responsibility for our own lives and needs. The spirit allies are not there to rescue us from this responsibility or to make life easy, but to help us be effective and in control of our life path. This they do with great wisdom and caring.

Replies from the spirit world are often metaphorical or symbolic in nature. We may see a flock of starlings fly past or feel the wind change direction, be shown an old castle door or a particular colour or scent. To understand these responses we have to look for the deep, poetic sense of what is being shown to us; that is not the same process as the logical analysis that we apply in everyday life.

Consulting the Medicine Wheel

One of the clearest ways of receiving reflections from the Web of Life is to use the Medicine Wheel as a mirror, consulting each Direction on a certain question. It takes a little practice to notice the responses that you get from the Directions; your mind may discount replies to start with, because it expects a certain answer – but this is rarely what you anticipate! Or you may distrust your intuition and the fleeting nature of information because it comes swiftly and passes you by, like flying birds or leaves on the wind. There is always a response from the Directions, if you approach the process with respect and an open mind and heart.

You may have a permanent Medicine Wheel set up outside that you can use, or you may prefer to build one indoors (see page 34). Whichever you choose, you will need enough space to position yourself outside of the Wheel at each Direction, facing towards the centre. You may wish to add extra decorations, such as fresh flowers, a candle at each Direction or objects to remind you of each element. For the South perhaps some leaves, for the West a pebble, feathers for the North and a candle for the East.

Medicine Wheel ritual

You will need: a candle; smudge-kit (see page 15).

To begin each session, place a candle in the centre, smudge yourself and the whole area, and then prepare yourself with silence, drumming, rattling or whatever creates a sacred space for you. Call in the Four Directions and light the candle when you are ready to begin.

To end each session, blow out the candle, thanking the Four Powers for their help and sending the light as a blessing to the Web.

FIRST SESSION

1 To familiarize yourself with the process of consulting the Medicine Wheel, sit in silence at the South point of the Wheel for at least three minutes, experiencing everything that you sense and getting a flavour of the medicine of the South Direction.

2 Move clockwise to the North and repeat step 1.

3 Move clockwise to the West and repeat step 1.

4 Move clockwise to the East and repeat step 1.

5 Take a few moments when this is complete to record your experiences: how each place felt, how you felt physically or emotionally in each one, what thoughts came to you, which Directions you wanted to stay in, which ones you wanted to move on from, and so on. Make written or pictographic notes or use an audio recording. Remember there is always a response when you ask in a sacred manner; if you experienced 'nothing', this is part of the information that you received. Nothing also has a feel and maybe even a colour or sound. On the many occasions when I have guided people through this process, I have never failed to wonder at the change that happens to their appearance as they sit at each Direction. Their whole physical bearing and tone of voice can change, without their realizing it, as they move around the Wheel.

SECOND SESSION

This session gives you the opportunity to ask the question 'What are my gifts?' Move around the Wheel as before, asking the question aloud at each Direction. This time you may like to make brief notes as you go, if this helps you to remember, but beware of writing in detail and losing your focus. Audio recording is less distracting, because the physical body is less engaged with this process.

Now the questions are up to you …

CHAPTER FIVE

Love and
Relationships

The Circle of Life

All life is born of spirit and matter, male and female. This coupling represents the primary vortex of potential and energy and is placed at the centre of the Medicine Wheel; from this position it symbolizes the great power source of the Web of Life, constantly dancing the spiral steps of Creation, constantly in motion. Creation is being physically birthed all the time, dies and is reborn in a never-ending sacred Circle of Life. This holds true for everything from the stars to microscopic life.

We can trace this continual genesis right back to the exploding matter of star substance at the birth of the Cosmos. Traditional myths have long described this cosmic birth with the same essential storyline that science now tells. We carry this story in some deep place of sacred recall within us. This birth memory unites all parts of Creation as relatives, as children of these primal opposites, both on our home world and on all the stars and planets.

How we are each in relationships with other humans, through the vehicle of our male and female forms, embodies the great cosmic dance. Through our choices and loves, our actions and reactions we send out harmony or discord, passion or indifference into the Web.

The relationship mirror

Facing the personal challenge of relationships in daily life offers the perfect classroom in which to learn about ourselves. Relationships take numerous forms, from those with intimate lovers to those with passing acquaintances. We ourselves play many roles, as mentor, carer, teacher, persecutor, lover and parent, using different settings to express and explore our human shapes. How we deal with these relationships is a powerful reflection of who we are and what lessons we are currently learning. If we can look at the patterns of our life experience we may get a sense of what lessons are being presented through them. Then we can deal with them in a way that enables us to move forward, rather than getting stuck in a repeating cycle of events and emotions.

'Coupledom'

When two people form an intimate relationship a 'coupledom' is formed. This has many facets, and its nature depends on the way we unite (and keep separate) our personal medicines. In a strong relationship this coupledom can alter shape and adapt as the two individuals change and grow. If such elasticity does not exist, then the individuals may be frustrated in their own growth and may even try to halt the natural life learning of their partner. Commitment to a process of evolving coupledom is therefore the best policy; commitment to the status quo can cause problems.

Although there is a romantic ideal connected with falling in love, the chemistry of passion is only one facet of the blending of the coupledom equation.

Sharing gifts

The long-term blending of the individuals' medicines shows how they manage the learning they are offering to each other through the relationship.

Mutual respect and the ability to communicate are essential ingredients in building and maintaining good relationships. We need respect for the parts of each other that we find less attractive or desirable, and we need to build trust by sharing who we really are. This is done in stages, of course, and there may always be some parts of ourselves that we need to keep private. One way to take stock of the elements in our own relationship jigsaw is to look at what gifts we have to offer. The following process can be adapted to any kind of relationship: romantic, business or one with friends or family. I shall use the example of a couple entering a long-term intimate partnership or marriage.

Creating a 'coupledom' map

1 Start by each consulting the Medicine Wheel (see page 84). This will help you both to find your personal medicine gifts. Make written or drawn notes of what you find so that you can remember them clearly. It is interesting to ask your partner at this point what gifts they experience you having at each Direction. Add these to your notes if it seems helpful.

2 Lay your personal 'maps' down side-by-side and discuss which gifts form natural bonds and which seem challenging or puzzling. Take it in turns to listen and be heard. Once the process has begun, there is no pressure to complete it quickly. Begin to sketch out a third 'coupledom' map, setting out your relationship expectations, hopes and strengths at each of the Four Directions. Let this discussion take as long as it needs – you may wish to keep coming back to it over a period of time. But the coupledom map is not a binding contract to be cited at times of disagreement, for both of you will change your own personal maps as you gather life experience.

3 This is a process that you can repeat over time, updating your relationship and finding out about its changing shape – and each others.

Looking at our legacy

Imagine, if you can, a really thick rope made of thousands of individual strands, stretching back through time – its origin beyond the powers of sight. You are one of the strands at the front end of the rope, which is slowly growing as it moves forward through the present moment towards the future. One day your strand will have reached its full length and will become an integrated fibre of this ancestral timeline, which will still be growing through the present into the future. Into this rope of humanity are twisted all the experiences, knowledge, mistakes and successes of those whose life threads make it up. It holds all the wisdom, ignorance, loves, hates, hopes and dreams of those lives and relationships. Each one of us leaves our legacy in this rope, passing on our experiences and becoming ancestors for those who follow.

In some Native American traditions there is a wise teaching that tells us we should be constantly mindful of the consequences of our actions and choices – not just for our children or grandchildren, but for the next *seven* generations. This means not only the effect on our personal bloodline, but on *all* our relations: the creatures, the stones, the waters. And it goes beyond physical ecology, where the consequences of our actions are becoming increasingly obvious. How will we handle information and facts and pass them on? Will we build communities that are peaceful and compassionate in their structures or ones that are fearful and destructive? Will our creativity and vision brightly colour the future, or will our children inherit inventions and discoveries that cause havoc?

This way of looking at what kind of a thread we weave into the time-rope is a simple and powerful yardstick for living in balance and beauty. Of course we cannot know for certain what the outcomes will be, but an awareness of this 'law of legacy' is much needed in today's 'live-for-the-moment' world. After all, seven generations ago our ancestors' actions shaped the present-day world. In Chapter Eight there is a ritual to send positive thoughts and blessing to these seven generations (see page 139).

The fourfold family circle

Many people influence our lives – some in a fleeting way, others for many years. There are some people whom we never meet and who never know us but who nevertheless have a profound influence on who we are. They become part of our inheritance: the strand that we weave into life.

The family of our birth (whether we know them or not) gives us our genetic lineage, our bloodline. Through our birth parents our soul receives a gateway to existence, enabling it to materialize in physical form for this earthwalk. We may share our birth parents with others – our brothers and sisters. This family tree branches into the future and has roots in the past. We can think of this as our family of the West Direction.

Our friends are our family of the heart – our South Direction family – whom we choose for ourselves. This family may change over time, but as life goes on we choose those with whom we can share from the heart, with whom we can play, laugh and love. It may be that we rarely meet them, but these are people with whom we have built up a measure of trust.

Teachers and mentors influence us as we are growing up and throughout life. This North Direction family consists of those who directly teach us or who record information that 'speaks' to us. Such information touches our lives in all kinds of ways: spiritual, political and philosophical. Our teachers may be living or dead, but they pass knowledge down through the generations to weave into our experience of being.

Inspiration, vision and passion are the concerns of our East Direction family, which is made up of writers, artists, musicians, film-makers – those who offer us a chance to share their creative experience. This family also includes those with whom we play in the 'spirit space' of colour, sound and imagination and those with whom we share passion.

Some people will appear in more than one Direction. For instance, a blood relative can also be a dear friend; a teacher may also be one whose work has inspired us; a close friend may also be a passionate playmate. When you enter into a partnership with another person, this fourfold family circle comes with you. The other person also sits in their own fourfold family circle, so when you are sharing your family backgrounds, don't forget to introduce everyone in the fourfold circle, for they are all part of who you are.

Signs of commitment

When you wish to make a long-term commitment to a partner or declare a marriage, a very simple and beautiful tradition is that of creating a sacred marriage bundle. Gather objects that symbolize your relationship, with both of you contributing items of special significance to you. Take your time, discussing what to include and what to leave out, exploring together your expectations, hopes and dreams. You will need a piece of natural fabric or soft leather to wrap the bundle in, and some cord or leather thonging to tie it together (this can be decorated with beads or feathers). Make everything as beautiful as you can. The number of items that you include (see box for suggestions) has no bearing on the power of the bundle – that is created through the power of your own minds and hearts and through the blessing of Spirit.

You may wish others to be present to witness your bundle's dedication, when the finished bundle should be smudged and offered to Spirit with prayers for its safekeeping. Bundles can be used for any circumstance where we wish to express a sacred intent, to bring blessings to a person, place or undertaking. So a bundle might be created to welcome and protect a newborn infant, to bless a house, help a business prosper or for safety on a long journey.

Traditional bundle items

- Lavender for sweetness
- Cedar or sage for cleansing
- Turquoise for protection
- Coral for blessings
- Natural tobacco leaf to please the spirits.

Creating a marriage bundle

You will need: symbolic objects; piece of natural fabric or leather; cord or leather thonging; beads or feathers (optional); smudge-kit (see page 15).

1 When everything is ready, smudge or cleanse everything you are to use, plus yourselves and any witnesses whom you may have asked to be present. Call in the Powers of the Four Directions, your sacred parents, your spirit allies and any other powers that you are used to working with. Never call in an aspect of Spirit on a whim or to impress yourself or others. This would not be acting respectfully and you might be taught a cautionary lesson.

2 You may wish to make declarations to each other as you place the items on the cloth or after you have wrapped them up and tied them with the cord. In the sacred space of ritual, speak simply from the heart, the best truth you know, trusting Spirit to show you the words you need.

3 When the process is complete and the bundle is 'joined', hold it up together and ask Spirit to give it – and your relationship – blessing and protection.

Bundle keeping

Once a bundle is joined, it has a spirit form as well as a physical one. Keep it safe and treat it with respect – after all, it represents your relationship! Bundles may be opened every so often to remind yourselves of the contents and of the intention they hold. Items may be taken away or added from time to time, reflecting the development of your relationship. If the intention for it no longer exists, a bundle should be dismantled in a respectful way and the items in it smudged to remove your intent, then returned or handed on.

Adopting a relative

This ritual creates a special bond between two friends who wish to make a lifelong commitment to each other, in effect forming a blood brother–sister, brother–brother or sister–sister bond. Take some time to discuss this step carefully, considering all its implications. It is not to be undertaken lightly. It is based on the Lakota Sioux sacred rite of Hunkapi – one of the sacred rites given to them by the holy figure of White Buffalo Calf Woman, who also brought them the sacred pipe ceremony.

Some questions that you might like to consider are: why do you feel the need to make this commitment? How will being 'relatives' change your present relationship? What do you expect to receive from your new relative? What are you not prepared to offer each other? How much will you involve your own blood families in the ritual? Do you expect others to accept your new relative as a full family member? Do you wish to make any legal arrangements regarding wills and so on? How do you want to express and formalize your new bond? Will your joining ritual be a public celebration? How will your other close friends react?

Formalizing the bond

When you feel you have explored the step you are about to take, you need to create the ceremony of adoption. Here are a few possibilities:

- Plan a quiet feast for the two of you at home, with plenty of flowers, decorations and candles.
- Go to a beautiful wild place in nature, perhaps camping out, and spend some quiet time, separately reflecting on your forthcoming adoption before coming together at the end of the vigil and building a sacred fire to symbolize the warmth and unity of your relationship. Do the fire ceremony together (see page 39) to offer up your hopes and ask for Spirit's blessing.
- Exchange gifts in a sacred ritual to celebrate your new relationship.
- Make a sacred bundle (see opposite).

Dismantling a relationship and moving on

How you manage dismantling a relationship and separating will depend on the circumstances and the kind of relationship that is ending. Even if you feel glad that it is over, you may like to consider one of the following rituals as a shamanic tidying-up process. They can be used at any time – even years after the parting, if it feels necessary.

Cutting the ties

This ritual can be done together, or just by one person. If your partner does not agree with the separation, you can take responsibility for your side of it with this ritual. There is no animosity directed at your partner, and a blessing for future peace and happiness is left at his or her 'feet' and at your own.

You will need: two short sticks (not from the same tree); personal symbolic items; a short length of red cotton, wool or silk thread; smudge-kit (see page 15); scissors; sage or another healing gift; two blessing gifts.

1 Find two sticks to symbolize you and your partner (if you are doing this ritual together, you can each find your own stick and adapt the process accordingly).

2 Tie something that represents you as an individual onto 'your' stick, and something that represents your partner onto the other. Do not use anything that you feel represents your coupledom or is closely associated with it.

3 Take the red thread and tie one end to your stick and the other end to your partner's.

4 Find a quiet place outside (not your garden) and stand each stick side-by-side in the ground. Smudge them and take a moment to visualize them representing you and your partner.

5 Cut the thread close to each stick and bury it in the space between them. Leave sage or a healing gift where you have buried it.

6 Place your blessing gift for your partner on the ground beside his or her stick and take your stick from the ground.

7 Walk on until you find a spot that feels light and harmonious, and plant your stick there. Leave your blessing gift and walk away into your new life. Do not look back or revisit these places in the next few weeks. Alternatively, you can take your stick home and decorate it with beautiful beads, ribbons or whatever feels celebratory and strengthening. Leave it on your personal altar or carry it with you for a while. You can even have a celebration feast, with it (you) as the honoured guest!

Gathering yourself together

We can give away parts of our soul essence without realizing it, often through phrases such as 'we'll always be part of each other' or 'my heart is yours'. These soul parts belong with you and cannot benefit anyone else. This ritual will gently encourage them to return. Where there is extensive soul loss (see page 46) a soul retrieval may be necessary; you need to have this done by an experienced shamanic practitioner.

You will need: a white candle; bird feather (optional); smudging herbs (see page 15).

Say a few words aloud, explaining to any absent parts of your essence that you will take care of them and keep them safe and that you really want them back now, so that you can feel strong and happy.

1 Find a time and place where you will not be disturbed.

2 Using a finger or feather as a pointer, trace a circle clockwise on the floor, large enough to sit in comfortably. This is your own sacred space and nothing and no one else is allowed to enter it. Smudge yourself, the candle and the space.

3 Enter the circle and sit down. Focus using the cross-and-circle exercise (see page 47) or any other focusing method that works for you. Keep checking that your attention has not wandered off. If it does, simply repeat the exercise and continue.

4 Light the candle and say:
'With this light I gather my soul and welcome it home.'

5 Sit quietly, drum or sing, and let your inner self be filled with the light of the candle. If memories of your relationship come to you, allow them to pass through your heart and mind without distracting you. Continue for as long as you can keep your focus, but no longer than fifteen minutes.

6 When you are ready to finish, pass your fingertips through the candle light and bring them to whatever part of your body feels right. Repeat this as many times as you wish, feeling the fire-spirit energy filling every corner of you with warmth and well-being.

7 Blow out the candle saying, 'For all my relations'. Keep the candle to use again if you wish to repeat this ritual.

8 Undo the circle by reversing your original pointing. Smudge the area and yourself.

9 When soul parts return, so can lost memories and emotions. Be gentle with yourself, and give yourself the support and time you need to integrate and love your new, and more complete, self.

The power of communication

Council circle rules

- Everyone sits in a circle so that all participants are equal.
- Each person speaks in turn, without interruption, moving clockwise around the circle.
- What happens in council is usually confidential, unless stated otherwise.
- If necessary, someone can be appointed to remind individuals of the rules, should they stray from them.
- Everyone should speak their own truth as best they know it and try to keep to what they are experiencing, without judging or blaming others.
- There can be any number of 'rounds', either pre-agreed or until a resolution is reached.

For any relationship, good communication is vital. Without it, resentment can build up as those involved get more and more out of touch and practical organization may dissolve. Lack of communication is a major cause of difficulties for couples, families, educators, carers and business organizations. It brings stress and alienation in its wake. If we do not listen to each other, we are simply storing up trouble.

Couples, families and work teams can all benefit from holding 'council circles'. For traditional tribes, council is a sacred space, representing a sharing and peace-making process. So a prayer or blessing is often made before starting the council, asking for Spirit's help and support. A 'talking stick' is normally used. The speaker holds the talking stick, then passes it on to indicate that he or she has finished. It is surprising how holding on to something gives you the courage to speak! An object that is visibly progressing around the circle also helps those who are impatient (especially younger members of the circle) to know that they will have their say.

But be warned: council is an ancient ceremony and a sacred one. You often find yourself saying unexpected things when you hold the stick – the process has a way of revealing truths and insights unlike any other process I know. Spirit certainly does play a powerful part at times. Telling your innermost feelings and thoughts to others, even close partners, may be a completely new experience. You may find that when it is your 'speaking' time, you feel it is right to remain silent and enjoy the support and respect of the circle instead.

Remember the times when you felt unheard, as if your view was unimportant or invalid – whether this was at school, in your childhood home, in adult relationships or at work? Being listened to fully, perhaps after many years, can be a thought-provoking and deeply healing process.

It may take time to find the courage to speak and gain trust in the circle and some people find it easier to begin by sharing their reluctance or shyness. No judgements are passed on what is said – or not said. Council is very different from open discussion and the offering of solutions is best avoided.

Making a talking stick

You will need: a stick; feathers, natural decorative materials such as wool, paint, coloured beads or threads.

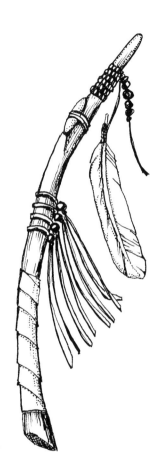

1 You need no special skills to make a talking stick and there are no rules; you simply take a stick and decorate it with items of your own choosing, such as feathers or beads. You may peel off the bark, carve the stick or find a beautiful piece of driftwood that needs no further decoration.

2 Make your talking stick as lovingly as you can, focusing on thoughts of harmony and peace while you are working on it. Have relaxing music playing or choose a time of day when you can be quiet and hear the sounds of birds or the silent song of the stars. When objects are made in this kind of environment – in a sacred manner – they absorb the atmosphere, energy and intent that you are investing in them.

3 You can keep your talking stick for many years. I have one that has powerful medicine and that has given quite a few people the courage to speak – perhaps for the first time ever – of what they fear, hope for or dream.

Preparing for a child

Conception is not just a mechanical biological event; it offers a gateway to enable a soul that is not yet in a body to pass through to a fresh experience of physicality. By actively preparing for the coming of a child, you send a signal to waiting souls.

Clearing the way

In today's nuclear family there is greater pressure than ever on the individual to 'get it right' in parenting terms and less experienced help around in the form of family advice and support, so becoming a parent may be quite a daunting prospect. You may not even recognize your fears and doubts, but such underlying feelings could inhibit conception.

Try sharing your fears with your partner in a sacred space, with Spirit's support. Enter the silence together (see page 19), call in the Four Directions (see page 23) and then write lists of your fears, which you can then share. You both need to be heard and to hear; automatic reassurance is not the answer, no matter how loving it is. Emotions may need to flow, and it is no help if the person who is trying to give support stuffs a metaphorical cork in your emotional bottle as soon as you have found the courage to remove it. Being honest with yourself, and with each other, represents a strong start in sharing the responsibilities of being parents. You can then burn your lists with some sage, releasing your fears to Spirit for help and release.

If you are a single parent, find someone you trust to share your fears with, or go out into nature and speak to Mother Earth. Dig a hole in a quiet place and speak into it. Say how you feel, your hopes and fears – *all* your feelings. When you have finished, pour a water offering into the hole and fill it up again. Place some sage over it, and perhaps plant some seeds as a heartgift.

Day of vigil

It may be that you did not have a good experience of mothering or fathering as you grew up, so you do not have a parenting blueprint that you feel you can use. If this is the case, spend a day of vigil in nature, with the intention of finding out what your strengths as a parent may be and how you can create a blueprint that is right for you (some of which may come from parts of your own experience that *have* worked). Ask Mother Earth and Father Sky to teach you what you need to know and feel their support and wisdom, which are always available if you ask for them.

The gift of a child

After conception

The mother-to-be should not do any sacred or ritual work, other than say prayers and make offerings, during pregnancy. Ask Mother Earth for an easy and safe delivery, good timing, strong health – whatever you feel concerned about. Walk often in nature and let yourself feel part of the great process of life. Touch the earth and smudge regularly. This will help you to connect to the coming child and the birthing process.

Connect with your baby from the very start by setting aside a special relaxation time each day to talk and sing to the new soul you carry beneath your heart. As the birth approaches, tell it how much you are looking forward to seeing it and all about the family that is waiting to welcome it. After the birth babies do recognize tunes they have heard in the womb, so use one or two simple songs (lullabies and nursery rhymes are fine) that you and your baby can associate with the quiet, loving energy of these times together. Fathers can join in too, and are usually in a better position to continue the voice-link during labour and birth. In native tribes music and chants are often used as part of the birthing and midwifery process.

You may like to choose a stone that will act as a companion right through to the birth, asking it to hold the qualities that you wish for, and perhaps letting it soak up energies that you would like to be present, such as starlight, sunshine, moonlight, bird song, recorded music and so on. Keep the stone close to you for support; even hold it during the birth if this is appropriate. Afterwards give it your thanks and return it to its home in nature.

In many cultures a newborn baby is taken outside the morning following the birth and presented to the earth and sky, the Four Directions or the sun. This is done by different members of the community, depending on local tradition, but usually by an elder or a grandparent, or the father or mother.

Make an offering as soon as possible after the birth to thank Mother Earth for her help. You may also wish to make a more ceremonial gesture of thanksgiving, perhaps linked to a naming, following the Native American tradition of the Giveaway. A Giveaway ceremony can be made to express any kind of thanks for the blessing of life.

The Giveaway

You will need: gifts (see below).

1 Gather together gifts, large or small: anything from a candle to a costly rug. It is good if you can make at least some of the gifts yourself, offering prayers and remembering your intention for the Giveaway as you do so. It is customary for people who know what you are doing to offer items for your collection to help you, but equally you can gather them yourself.

2 When you have prepared the gifts, distribute them to anyone you feel is right to receive them: acquaintances, close friends, family; simply be guided by your heart. This can be done individually, explaining why you are making your Giveaway, or at a gathering specially called for the purpose.

'Who are you?'

The name we give a new child is very important. The energy sound and meanings associated with it will be reflected to him or her whenever it is said. In native cultures a child is often named according to events that happened during conception or birth or from a sense of its spirit being. This spirit being is so strong that it is almost visible in the first few hours after birth, before the baby becomes tied to physicality and the spirit presence fades.

Throughout the child's upbringing, from its first breath (and even in the womb), parents need to ask gently 'Who are you?', with loving curiosity and respect. One of the greatest gifts we can give a child is to foster its self-esteem and awareness of itself as a unique and valuable human being, with gifts that are needed in the great Web of Life and with access at all times to the support and greater wisdom of its sacred parents.

It can be difficult to bring up a child within a culture whose systems do not always operate out of respect for life. As the child enters the wider society beyond the confines of family life, it sometimes seems that a materialistic and speed-obsessed worldview holds sway over them. A natural knowledge of the sacred can seem to be submerged under peer pressure and short-term thinking and action. But the perspectives and heart-connection that the child first experienced from its parents are planted deep within its life-soil and at the end of the day will, hopefully, win through as the only framework that actually makes sense and brings lasting well-being.

Presentation of a new baby

'Father Sky, Mother Earth, we come to you with thanks for this gift of new life, knowing that you are her/his true parents. May she/he be free of anything that is not part of her/his true being at this time. You have given her/him into our care, help us to take care of her/him in body and spirit. May she/he be blessed with good health, long life and may she/he walk in beauty.'

CHAPTER SIX
Indoor Living Spaces

The spirit of place

We sometimes forget that there are more occupants of a space than simply the visible human ones. The spirit of place is just one of the invisible presences around us all the time. We may become momentarily aware of this when we are sitting quietly by our fireside late in the evening and feel a companionable sense of the 'house' around us, or when we are driving through the countryside and a hill suddenly attracts our attention with its beauty, power and vastness.

Creation is watched over by a system of spirit keepers, who work in both wild and urban places. Different cultures around the world have had different names for these spirit presences, but whether they are known as gatekeepers, *devas* or *apus*, it has been recognized that many separate entities coexist in every location. There is a spirit associated with each type of place, from a tiny natural spring to a vast mountaintop.

A shaman is very aware of the importance of good relationships with the spirit of the places that he or she inhabits or works in. In traditional societies the shaman is often called upon to negotiate with the spirits involved when new buildings or roads are planned. If the history of a place has been violent or unhappy, then it may need spirit healing and its memories releasing before harmony can be restored. This can be done by using specific shamanic techniques and ceremonies that have common forms all over the world.

At a domestic and workplace level, the spirit of place may help explain why some houses are 'happy' and always full of life and people and why some business sites are sought-after because they have a prosperous track record. It also accounts for the reputation for 'bad luck' that certain places have. We can communicate with these energy beings, however, and give them explanations and apologies where appropriate, just as we would with human neighbours.

Just as you will find a new place unfamiliar and will take a while to get used to it, so the place itself needs to get used to you. When you move into a new home or workplace, treat its spirit with respect and introduce yourself as you would to a new neighbour, telling it what you plan to do in the place and of your wish for harmony during your time there. Make a goodwill offering – perhaps lighting a candle, playing gentle music, burning incense or whatever feels right to you.

Likewise, when you move out of a place, tell its spirit what is happening and bid it farewell and wish it a good relationship with whoever comes next; leave a thanks offering for the time you have spent there.

Keeping the boundaries

The energy field of a home space needs shamanic maintenance, just as our individual auras do. Whether you live in a city bedsit or a country cottage you need to keep the boundaries of your own personal living space clearly defined.

Energy is not restricted by physical barriers, so it can travel through walls, floors and ceilings. Therefore you need to construct a 'magic skin' in sacred space, just as you did for your own aura, covering the *entire outside* of your personal home space. It follows the same principles as the outer skin of your human aura (see page 72), allowing blessings and positive energies through and filtering out negatives.

If your home physically adjoins others (as in an apartment block or terrace), then the boundary membrane should be placed around all the party walls, ceilings and floors. The aim is not to confront or challenge your neighbours but to hold your *own* space in a balanced and confident way and be happily self-contained, rather than putting up siege defences!

This membrane may have a great deal to filter, especially if you live in a crowded and noisy situation. If you feel this is the case, create an automatic cleansing system that keeps the outer face of the magic skin clean – like a periodic shower of cleansing water to rinse it – or visualize it bathed in bright, purifying sunshine.

If you wish to mark your boundary on a physical level, you can do so with normal household decorating paint, using it either outside or inside and focusing your intention on marking the actual boundary. White is a traditional protective colour, as is red, but any hue can be chosen and designated for boundary marking, combined with a simple prayer. Reinstate these boundaries regularly with smudge, light, sound or whatever works most easily and effectively for you.

The threshold

Our front door and doorstep reflect the qualities of the space that lies beyond, the way it is maintained and the kind of people who live there. A well-lit, cheerful doorstep adorned with flowers or evergreens is welcoming, whereas one with empty, broken flowerpots and peeling paintwork gives a quite different message. This threshold is the place where the wider world ends and we enter our own personal territory. Whether it is marked by a simple cottage door or an elaborate, imposing one, people the world over have recognized the need to protect and strengthen this threshold, the boundary between private and public worlds.

In energy terms a threshold is a 'between' place, a liminal space where different realities touch. This may be the private–public meeting marked by the doorstep, the sea–land space of the shore or the liminal spaces in time, such as twilight or dawn when day and night meet, or the end of the old year and start of the new. These are places where our awareness adjusts and where there is, therefore, a natural pause in reality. There is a need to define and protect these thresholds, and traditions abound in every culture relating to front entrances. The nomadic yurt dwellers of Asia carry beautifully carved front doors around with them, complete with frames, while Indian homes sport colourful painted symbols around the door and auspicious patterns are chalked daily on the doorstep. In some parts of England the custom of whitening doorsteps persists and a horseshoe or other iron ornament may be hung over the door to prevent fairies from entering the house. Pelmets and fringes above doorways and windows both protect from bad luck entering and bless those who cross the threshold. In some Native American traditions protection is added by marking all the doors and windows with the ash of burnt oak.

One old British protection ritual involves taking a small quantity of ale to a rowan tree and pouring it at the foot of the tree as an offering, asking the tree for its blessing. Then two or three twigs are picked (without using a knife) and bound together in a cross with red ribbon. This is then placed to your forehead, then to your heart, and then you kiss it. It is taken through all the rooms in the house, circling each one with it held aloft in front of you, after which you walk backwards through the front door and tie it above the door frame. To keep the protection refreshed, it is supposed to be repeated every equinox and solstice.

In any ritual remember that it is not the use of a particular 'charm' or spell that creates an effect but the power of your own intent. Traditional rituals use symbols and substances that have appropriate sacred and medicine associations, but it is the person focusing their intent that weaves the real magic.

Caring for your threshold

- Smudge the front door and doorstep regularly.
- Hang a bunch of smudging herbs above your door.
- Keep your threshold and front step swept clean and washed.
- Paint your doorstep white or red (both are protective colours).
- Plant an evergreen in a tub or in the ground on either side of your doorway to mark the line of your threshold.
- Place a large stone on each side of your doorstep to mark the threshold line, asking them to bless all who enter.
- Hang a decorative ribbon or cloth pelmet above your door to act as an energy filter.

The power of cleanliness

The first time I really noticed the effect that tidiness has on energy was when I was staying in a tepee. These wonderful conical tent homes of the Native North American Plains people have a central fire inside, and the smoke is drawn up through an efficient draught system, to escape through a smoke hole at the top. However, if a tepee is not tidy, the smoke begins to misbehave and fill the space; when the confusion has been sorted out – whether it stems from scattered belongings or disruptive emotions – one can literally see the energy clearing.

Taking this principle indoors to our own homes, we can see how tidying and cleaning attract positive energy into our living and working spaces. When housework is seen in this light, it can become a sacred celebration of harmony rather than a dreary chore. Do it in a sacred manner and with a light heart: vacuum with a song or by moving in a simple rhythm; handle the objects you dust with thoughts of thanksgiving for the gifts you have in your life; move things around the room until it feels harmonious; wash windows in celebration of the light and warmth from the sun. And remember that by using the minimum of cleaning chemicals you respect the body of Mother Earth and do not contribute to pollution.

To honour the spirit of your home or workplace, set aside a small table or suitable space for a house-blessing shrine. On the shrine place something from each realm: plant, mineral, creature and fire (represented by a candle or oil lamp). Choose items that you find pleasurable to look at and that make a harmonious whole as a group. Care of the shrine will become a regular 'sacred housework' ritual as you set out fresh flowers or tend a plant, wash a stone or crystal and light the candle or lamp with a simple prayer for the harmony of the living space and all who dwell in it.

Changing life habits

As we grow and change so does the way we behave in daily life. Whenever we make personal changes and find new ways of seeing life, as we do when we start to follow a shamanic path, we may wish to express these inner changes in new living habits. This does not mean, of course, that we go to the extreme of posting revisionist house rules on the front door, although it is only human to wish to share our discoveries with those around us. Finding out how to express these discoveries in everyday ways is an important part of grounding and integrating our new learning.

Relating to the world through the shamanic perspective you will naturally approach your domestic and work tasks in new ways, as part of the sacred process of living. Your living spaces will become increasingly aligned with the natural energies of the Web and you will find new patterns of behaviour emerging. A growing sensitivity to the part the spirit of place plays in these spaces, whether home or workplace, will create a partnership in which harmony and balance are the underlying principles.

So as you try out new habits of living, whether it is building an altar, blessing your threshold or doing your daily morning ritual, be aware of the change in the personal shape you present to the world. It is as if you are a jigsaw piece and your friends, family and colleagues are used to your being a certain shape. As you change, for whatever reason, this shape changes and you need to find a new 'fit' with the people and places around you. Some of the 'old' life will not adapt and friendships, activities – even your choice of home or work – may change too. This is all part of the natural process of losses and gains that applies throughout life. Because each of us is unique in the way we deal with change, all we can do is honour our own needs and allow ourself, and those around us, time to adjust.

With your new shamanic awareness come new sacred responsibilities in relation to the maintenance of the energy of your environment. As you seek to express respect for the sacred into your daily life and to find ways to honour natural harmony and integration with the Web, so you will bring change to all that your shape touches in an organic and gentle way. Experiment with small steps, consider those suggestions shown here, consult the spirit of place and listen to your intuition, which will suggest more.

Honouring your home

- Remove your shoes at the front door to mark and respect the different space within your home.
- Have a 'quiet' place in the house for sanctuary and reflection where anyone can go to reflect and be undisturbed in an atmosphere of peace.
- Settle serious conflict by using a talking stick (see page 97).
- Say a blessing, or offer up a quiet moment of thanks, before eating.
- Have an agreed time when everyone in the house meets for a social catch-up.
- Light a candle or make an offering for the healing and well-being of your ancestors.
- Cleanse the threshold each morning before anyone passes over it or last thing at night.
- Hang a wind chime near your front door where you can ring it each time you go out or come back in to bring blessings to the home.

Clear and balanced living spaces

If a room feels oppressive or tense, this may be because heavy energies have built up and have been unable to clear naturally. The atmosphere in any room can feel disturbed if strong emotion, for instance, has either been expressed or withheld there; if someone with an untidy or ungrounded energy field has been in the room; if there has been a lot of mental concentration; or if aggressive or intense music and films have been played in it.

It is therefore important to keep the energy of our homes and workplaces balanced and clear. We have already explored useful energy-clearing methods such as drumming and rattling, but there is a further 'energy-plumbing' method that I find extremely useful.

Making an energy-dispersal system

You can build an energy-dispersal system that operates constantly to take away surplus, grubby or highly charged energies that may have accumulated in a room. Use the wonderful power of your imagination, coupled with the intent of your mind, to construct this outlet to keep home and workplace calm and clear.

1 Imagine a point in the centre of the floor like a drainage outlet with pipework leading from it to carry the energies away outside and into the earth, as if it were leading to a soakaway.

2 With your imagination, place a one-way valve on the outside end of the outlet so that the flow of energy can go in only one direction, *away* from the house and *into* the earth.

3 Ask permission from Mother Earth for this and explain what you are doing. Leave a heartgift outside to show your gratitude. The outlet will remain in operation all the time, to keep the energies of the room clear. As you are programming the drain only to take out surplus or negative energies, do not be concerned that the room (or those using it) will be 'drained' of vitality in any way, for when you are in a balanced energy environment you will feel lighter and more relaxed.

4 Every so often imagine that the outlet and valve are being cleared and cleaned. This can be done either in the room itself or from your indoor power place. Enter the silence (see page 19) and imagine this process happening; you may see a pressure washer, use a sonic wave or a beam of light – whatever works best for you. Construct this energy outlet in an office, workshop, therapy room, gymnasium, studio, sickroom, nursery or classroom (in fact, anywhere it is needed).

Taking stock of the elements

Earth, air, wind and fire play an important role in creating a positive indoor space. Imbalance can come about when there is too much or too little of an element present. The remedy lies in adjusting the amount of the element in question or in balancing the other elements. Here are a few common examples of such remedies to help you take stock of your own environment.

The presence of underground water is often noticeable during very wet weather, when the occupants may feel muddled, hyperactive or even depressed. This requires the expert attention of a dowser, crystal healer or other alternative practitioner who can work with underground springs and streams. As a temporary remedy, construct a membrane with your intent (see page 105), completely covering the underside of your house to filter out any negativity, surges or imbalances of energy.

Air may be present in unwanted draughts, in the feeling of being too exposed to the winds or vulnerable to the gaze of passers-by. Make living rooms more cosy with heavy curtains and create spaces within the house where you feel enclosed and private. If the air in your home is getting stale or stuffy or the occupants feel restless (as before a thunderstorm) even when there is adequate ventilation, you may need to remove static by misting the room with water or by burning candles. Smudging and incense are also powerful remedies, and frankincense can be helpful in deepening and relaxing your breathing.

If a building has too much earth energy it can become oppressively still. The occupants may become overly introspective and stuck in patterns of behaviour. The traditional fire in the hearth will lift the atmosphere; alternatively, candles will invite in fire energy to balance the excess of earth energy. Good, bright lighting and warm colour schemes will also help. Mirrors can be used effectively to reflect sunlight into the space, and maximum light should be allowed in through all the windows and doors.

A house where the fire element is unbalanced may feel either overheated and intense or cold and dead. Reality within the house may seem thin or dreamlike. Timekeeping may be difficult, and practical tasks may seem overwhelming. This environment needs earthing – literally. Bowls of pebbles placed around the home and a focus on the activities of food and bathing areas will bring harmony and grounding. Sacred or creative activity should be kept within strict physical and time boundaries, or even done in a more naturally grounded environment.

The gift of food

Eating patterns for much of the world's population have changed radically within the lifetime of a single generation. Whereas in the past we mostly ate food produced from the soil, climate and spirit keepers of our native land, we now absorb the energies of many lands through an incredible variety of foodstuffs.

I can remember my grandfather bringing freshly dug vegetables in from the garden, to be cooked just minutes before they were needed. Now carrots or sweetcorn may have been placed in the freezer weeks before we use them, and who knows how long or far they may have travelled to get there? Furthermore, our food sources may not have been grown and produced in accordance with their natural seasons. Summer fruits are now available in winter, and growing seasons are continually being lengthened by genetic intervention and technological advances. This means that the patterns and cycles of the medicine gifts of different plants may no longer synchronize with our bodies' needs.

We have no way of knowing the outcome of this on seven generations, but we can maintain a sacred attitude to food, as a gift from Mother Earth – no matter how it reaches us; we can remember to bless it and give thanks for it.

Sacred gathering

Whether you shop in a local store or large supermarket, 'pick' food from the shelves as you would from your own garden. Look at the experience of shopping not as a hurried chore, but as hunting, harvesting and gathering. These primal activities have happened somewhere on your behalf, so as you collect what you need, offer the ancient hunter's prayer of thanks to all your relations that have given of themselves so that you can live. And thank the human lives who have played their parts in getting the food to you. This connects you to the gift of food in an appropriately respectful and sacred way.

When you have brought your food home, you can give thanks by lighting a candle set in a thanksgiving shrine in your kitchen. The shrine may be a small shelf or cupboard decorated with symbols of fruitfulness, the sun and the elements or the seasons, or it may be a simple candle in a beautiful holder, which is lit only when you are preparing food and eating.

The heart of the house

The kitchen is indeed the heart of the house, being a meeting place and a focus for the practical tasks of everyday living, such as cooking and laundry. Try some of the following suggestions to keep the kitchen and yourself in harmony with the natural rhythms and cycles and to make it a place for celebrating life:

- No matter how you dispose of your kitchen waste, ask Mother Earth to recycle it and make fertile what you no longer need.
- Place photos of your family and friends on a bulletin board in the kitchen or the place where you eat, to include them at your table.
- Buy food to supply your needs, not your fears.
- Choose foods that are in season in the land in which you are living.
- Wherever possible, buy food that has been grown organically and locally.
- Use the minimum of chemicals for cleaning and maintaining your home.
- Choose electrical appliances that offer minimal energy use and maximum efficiency.
- On a sunny day take a bowl of hand-washing outside, sit on the earth to wash it and let it dry in the breeze – an elemental celebration!
- Sing and dance in celebration of the beauty of the world as you work in your kitchen; men and women each have their special beauty to add to this.
- Pick a small vase of seasonal foliage, flowers or twigs, and keep it where you can see it to connect you to the natural cycles around you.

- Offer a small amount of the best of your food or pour the first drops of your drink (be it wine or tea) onto the earth, thanking Mother Earth for her gifts.
- Include other relatives in your feeding schedule, leaving food outside for the birds and any other creatures that you wish to have visit you; but first you might like to find out a few facts about who eats what, or you may be surprised by the visitors that call!

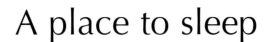

A place to sleep

Sleep is a time when our consciousness journeys into dreams and our body renews itself physically. Having a good quality of sleep is therefore essential to well-being on all levels. Where space is limited, however, the bedroom is often used for purposes other than simply sleep; it may also be used as a study or office, meditation area or television room.

If you have to use your bedroom for other activities, make sure that you designate a 'room within a room' around the bed area, to mark it out as a place of rest and renewal in which you can sleep peacefully and well. You can delineate this area physically with folding screens or curtains, or even by placing a large rug beneath the bed to extend beyond the area.

You can also mark out this sleeping sanctuary as a sacred space, drawing the boundary with your finger or a feather. Always mark such sacred spaces in a clockwise (sunwise) direction. A slightly more elaborate way to make this space really well-defined is to imagine it enclosed by three loops: draw the first loop going all around the outside horizontal plane of the bed; the second passing from the head of the bed over the top to the foot, and back underneath to the starting point; and the third loop goes from side to side of the bed, passing over the top and returning underneath to meet the starting point. This is a powerful ancient symbol for marking and protecting any space.

Make sure that the whole of your sleeping area or bed lies within the marked space and that no unnecessary disturbance enters that space, so that it is a place of rest and renewal for you. Do not place altars and crystals near the bed unless they are linked to your dreaming activities, as their energy fields could disrupt your sleep or trouble your dream state. Altars and crystals will, however, 'sleep' if you cover them with a cloth when you wish to rest. Electrical equipment, such as a hi-fi, computer or television, also gives out disruptive energy fields and needs to be unplugged to prevent this happening while you sleep.

Dreaming

Altars and crystals may be used in the bedroom if they are intended to help develop your dreaming skills in some way, or assist you in remembering your dreams. In this case, cover or dismantle them when you are not sleeping, or you will still feel connected to your dreaming energies when you want to be wide awake!

In some traditions, the owl is said to be bearer of dreams; in other traditions, it is the bear, the great winter-dreamer. Record your dreams in a journal or a

New Crystals

Crystals have an ability to absorb all kinds of energies, so a crystal that is new to you should always be cleansed first to release any undesirable energies that it may have already accumulated. You can do this by either leaving it outside on the earth overnight asking Mother Earth to cleanse it, or by immersing it in water to which you have added some sea salt.

dictation machine as soon as you wake. Place this where you can reach it with as little physical movement as possible, so that the gateway between the physical and dream worlds remains open until you have recalled your dreams. Interpreting the metaphors and symbolism within a dream is entirely personal. You can enter the silence in your power place to reflect on what these might mean. Notice if there is a pattern or recurring sequence in your dreams that may be reinforcing a certain message or insight.

Using crystals

When you use crystals in any sacred work always wash them first in sea-salt water to clean them. Then spend some moments holding them and explaining what you wish them to assist you with. This programs the crystal and it will continue to hold your request and work with it. Each kind of crystal (rose, quartz, citrine, amethyst, etc.) has its own natural strengths suiting it to particular kinds of requests and help. Clear quartz has an all-round energy that works well to amplify your intent. Wash them again after use and thank them for their help.

Size is not an indication of power in a crystal, and some tiny crystals can hold intent in a big way! Your working crystals may enjoy some rest and renewal time by sitting in the moonlight or sunshine (take care with rose quartz, though, as heat can cause it to fade). But do this well away from your sleep area. A friend who normally had no problem sleeping began to have restless nights at full moon until she realized that a large crystal was enjoying the moonlight on her bedroom windowsill and was amplifying the vibrant, wakeful moon energies!

Creating a bedroom altar

Your altar items need to be placed on a piece of cloth. You might include:
- Something representing a night bird such as the owl – perhaps a feather or a small carved figurine
- Some sage or sea salt for protection
- A piece of rose quartz or a herkimer diamond (a double-ended clear quartz crystal) to help with your dream recall and to prevent nightmares.

You can arrange your altar in a small wall cupboard, which has doors that can be closed when the altar is not in use. This is an excellent way of keeping your sacred items safe and your activities private, especially if you wish to put shrines in more public areas of your home, such as the hallway or kitchen.

A natural house

We have become accustomed to the effect that artificial and processed materials have on us, and in today's home we are generally surrounded by all sorts of plastic surfaces, paints, carpeting and so on. In shamanic terms, everything comes from Mother Earth, including all the creations and inventions of humankind – they have been made from her body, from natural materials. But when we go into a house where all the materials are in their natural forms we feel the difference. There is a special restfulness in such an interior, a down-to-earth quality that nourishes the soul; the contrast shows us how we have acclimatized to the background effect of manufactured materials. We have even become oblivious to the electromagnetic effect of our house's wiring circuit.

For some people the answer is to embrace alternative technologies wholeheartedly, but this is a hard path to follow, and this kind of total life change is usually an impossible prospect. But there is no reason why we should not be creative in finding out what *is* possible.

A gradual transformation

It is often most effective to approach change in a series of manageable steps, and to have fun along the way. So why not start to create a more natural lifestyle by making an inventory of your home environment, taking stock of how many manufactured materials and how much electrical equipment you have. It may not be possible to remove everything that you feel is 'un-natural' – and much of it has a practical place in today's busy world. However, you might consider making gradual adjustments to your home, to reflect and reinforce your growing shamanic awareness.

The easiest room to transform in this way is usually the bathroom. This is an elemental area anyway, with its prevalence of water energy, and although there may be electrical showers or heaters, it is probably the least 'wired' space in the house. It lends itself to decoration with natural materials: towel rails may be made of driftwood; large pebbles and shells can ornament windowsills and shelves; and of course bathing in plant essences by candlelight is quite magical.

Once you have established a more natural space somewhere in your home, using that area will give you pleasure, will remind you of the benefits of a natural home and will inspire you to extend the process. I have found that the keynote is pleasure: enjoy the changes, don't make it a worthy mission and it will stand a much greater chance of success!

Taking small steps

The following suggestions offer ways to bring your home into closer harmony with the natural world. Try some of them out and see how they feel. You can take them on as medicine tasks, done with all your shamanic senses stretched, and see how they alter the energy dynamics of your home or workspace. Monitor your feelings and energies before and after each step. By trying out some of these suggestions, I am sure you will feel inspired to experiment further and bring your living spaces into greater connection with the natural world.

- Make an 'air change' at a time when the air outside feels good and energized. Open all your windows and doors, and invite the blessings of this element in as you do so. As you close them again (after at least fifteen minutes), thank the air element for its help.
- Switch off all possible electrical equipment, including lights, for an hour or so. Sense the difference and let the house (and yourself) 'rest' from the electromagnetic energy fields created by the equipment.
- Go through old papers, clothes, books, toys, tapes and so on. Recycle, pass on or throw out anything you haven't used recently and don't need to keep. By holding on to objects you hold on to energy that is outdated.
- Liven up the sluggish atmosphere in a room by clapping a lively rhythm into all the corners and behind furniture, perhaps by singing some words that hold joy for you, in time with your clapping. Children love to join in with this.
- Find pictures or models of animals whose medicine you wish to call into your home: for instance, the beaver can help maintain the home; the wolf can guard it; the butterfly can transform its energy. Work with your intuition and notice which animals turn up on your doorstep, which animal images appear through your letterbox and in the gifts of friends once you have started your search.
- Place photographs or postcards of landscapes and wild places in rooms that feel cut off from these outdoor energies, especially if they have a limited outlook or very small window area.
- In the natural world there is always motion and change, and our indoor spaces can get very static, causing our senses to become dull. Have objects that create movement in your room: the flickering of candlelight, mobiles near a door or window or a glass crystal hanging where it catches the sunlight.

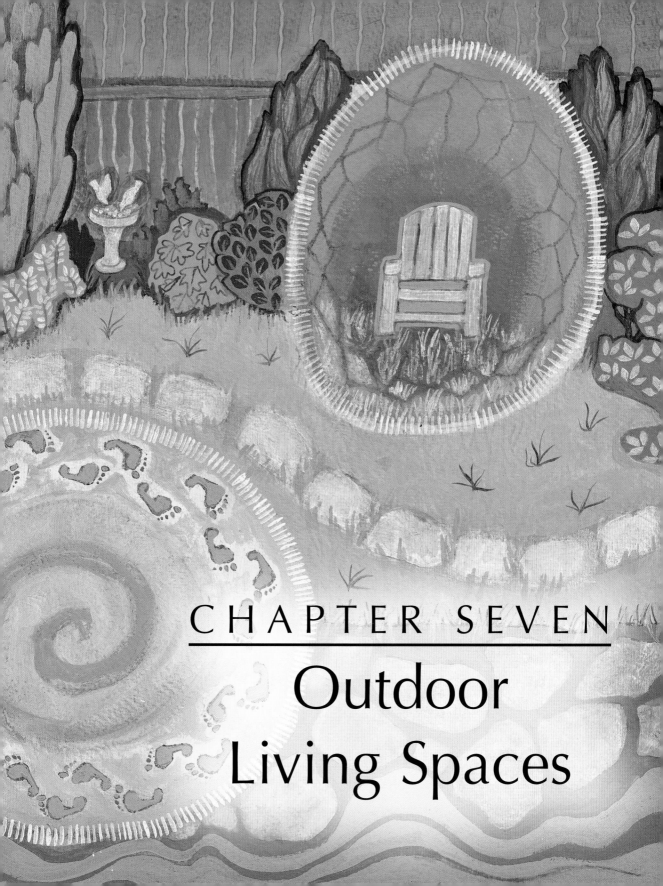

CHAPTER SEVEN
Outdoor Living Spaces

Heart and land

A shamanic connection with the land comes primarily from the heart. In terms of our personal Medicine Wheel, our first response to life comes from the emotional centre, at the South of the Wheel (see page 25). Without this heart response, fact-gathering by the mind at the North of the Wheel may not be enough to call us to action. We need to relate initially by *caring*.

As daily life in the developed world has moved further and further away from a connection with the natural world and with the Web of Life, so this has deeply affected our emotional centre. Our work and our everyday tasks no longer resonate with the rhythms of the natural cycle of the seasons, and our socializing has lost much of the ceremony and earth-celebration rites that enhanced not only our energies but those of the world around us. Little wonder then that stress and emotional disorders of the heart and mind are so prevalent today. The 'wild' natural being within each of us is bound to feel anger and frustration at having to spend life confined to unnatural environments and time constraints. Many traditional healers and teachers recognize the sorrow and loss created by this disconnection, which is buried deep within our communities.

Ecologists are also recognizing that we have reached a state of information overload. It is only when we come into personal contact with the natural world, when we hear the sap pumping through a tree in springtime or see and smell the damage done by oil on a coastline that this world becomes real for us and we feel in our hearts for our relatives' well-being. It is only by getting up close and personal with the land that we can heal and restore our hearts, there is no substitute for getting down on our hands and knees and watching iridescent beetles in our own backyard, feeling the wind on your face or listening to the birds calling at twilight.

The Place of Wonder

There is a need to enter into the wonder of a child for whom the world is new. Ceremony and ritual can bring us to this inner place of heart connection, and when we make any sacred objects we need to seek out this inner place of simple wonder.

A prayer arrow is a beautiful way of expressing our love and care for Mother Earth and Father Sky. It is not an arrow bearing aggression, but one symbolizing fertility, inviting the energy of Father Sky to penetrate into the soil body of Mother Earth to bring peace and blessing. As we make the prayer arrow, the meditative action of winding on bands of coloured thread reinforces our prayer for harmony and balance.

Making a prayer arrow

Some years ago I took part in an outdoor course that involved much ceremony and healing. It took place on a Welsh hill farm and many of these arrows were left dotted over the fields. The down-to-earth local farmers – far from seeing this as strange or intrusive – commented on how different the land felt afterwards: happier and more alive.

You will need: a strong, straight stick, the thickness of a finger and about 8–16 in (20–40 cm) long; brightly coloured threads; a few feathers; a sharp knife.

1 Work in an atmosphere of quiet and harmony. Cleanse yourself, your work area and everything you intend to use. Ask Spirit to guide your hands, and thank the relatives who have provided the materials you are to use. State your prayer intention aloud four times:

> 'May balance and beauty be with Mother Earth and Father Sky.'

2 Take the stick, remove the bark and sharpen one end. Focus on your prayer as you work, singing or talking to the stick as you do so, for a sacred object is a living thing.

3 Starting a short distance from the sharpened end, cover the wood by binding the threads closely together along it; let your hands guide you in choosing which colours you use, acting from your heart and intuition, not your mind. When you have nearly reached the end, lay the feather quills along the stick and use the last portion of thread to bind them in place, like a little crown. You can add a couple of feathers dangling from this end to invite the breeze to activate your prayer and please the spirits.

4 When the prayer arrow is finished, take it outdoors. Sense where the land wants it to be planted, then push it firmly into the soil, repeating your prayer. Touch the earth and dedicate your prayer stick to all your relations.

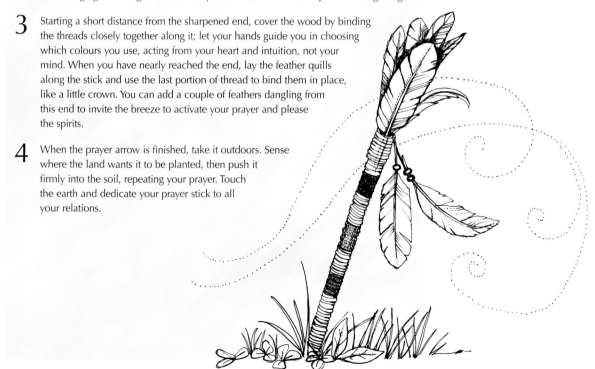

Keeping the boundaries

The land is crossed and recrossed with the tracks of many creatures that mark their territories. These tracks are mostly undetectable by human senses. They are also essentially trails of intent. There are human equivalents in fences, walls, rights of way and bridle paths. The way our land boundaries are marked in this physical sense often reflects our attitude to life and our personal relationships with other people. Do you have a high hedge all round your home or an open picket fence? What do you consider to be a threat to your boundaries and an invasion of your territory: a travelling salesman coming up the path, a visiting tomcat in the flowerbed or loud music from a nearby neighbour?

An ancient British tradition marked parish boundaries and kept them legally established by 'beating the bounds'. This annual event, still performed in some places, involves a procession all around the perimeter of the land covered by the parish. One way of reinforcing the energy boundary of your land is by walking around it regularly. This is also an excellent way to connect physically with the land of which you are 'keeper' at this time in its long history. You may make this boundary walk daily or once a year, but no matter how often it is done, it will remind you *and* the land just where your keeping extends to.

If there are gaps in the energy boundary, other energies may move in and (not so readily noticeable) energy from within may leak out. I learned this some years ago when I was keeper of a town garden, a hidden oasis of green surrounded by car parks and shopping areas. That summer, while the perimeter wall was taken down for repairs, the garden lost vitality and several large, previously healthy plants died. When the wall was eventually replaced, the plants' swift return to health was so noticeable that I realized how the energy of the garden had been leaking out through the gap in the wall. This could have been prevented, had I thought to visualize a spirit wall in place during the building work.

A spirit boundary can be marked with either water or stones that have been asked to hold your intent. If physically connecting with the land is impossible, make a diagram or map on paper which strongly outlines the boundary. This map can then be offered to Mother Earth by burying it in the ground, or to Father Sky in a fire ceremony (see page 39).

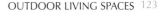

Cycles of creation

The two great lights that shine on Mother Earth – the sun and the moon – affect all that happens on the land and in the waters of our beautiful world. The moon creates the great movement of the tides, and as our bodies are largely made up of water, we too respond to this tidal effect. The light from the sun not only provides day and night, but also seasonal influences on our systems, which bring about physiological and emotional changes.

All aspects of the land and of ourselves take part in this dance of light and energy: weather systems, the growing patterns of plants, the spawning of coral reefs. Human responses to these variations of solar and lunar energy vary from person to person. For instance, some people feel like sleeping more in winter; others need very little sleep at full moon and are up with the owls. Our appetite for food, our physical energy levels, our capacity for mental activity – even our romantic passions – are affected by the shifting dance of energy around us. In traditional communities this dance is recognized and honoured through seasonal tasks, celebrations and rituals that link the energy of the whole community to these rhythms and to the land. Where these rhythms are communally honoured, human energy patterns begin to synchronize with the natural ones. A well-known example of this is when women living as a close group, perhaps working in the same office building, menstruate together and in time with the moon cycles to which menses are linked.

Knowing how our personal Medicine Wheel aspects of heart, mind, body and spirit are affected by these lunar and solar energies gives us invaluable information, which can help us to manage our energy, suiting our activities and plans to our energy peaks and troughs; this knowledge, and the sense of being in step with the sun and moon also connects us to the land that we share with them.

Finding out your own patterns in this dance of energy is quite easy but requires paying attention to your energy levels over a period of time. There are many ways to do this, but you might like to try using the two simple charts shown here: one for the moon and the other for the sun cycle. These form a graph, mapping your energy according to your personal Medicine Wheel aspects: South = emotions, North = mind, West = body and East = spirit. The longer you keep your records, the clearer the picture you will obtain. Merely by undertaking this regular act of monitoring your personal energy levels (although occasional lapses are only human!) you will be aligning yourself with the same rhythms as all of your relations.

Dancing with the sun and moon

Each chart follows the same form, using a strip of five parallel lines, rather like a musical stave – so a music manuscript book is ideal for these records. Relevant dates are marked out along the strip, according to whether you are recording the sun or the moon (see below). The energy level of each Medicine Wheel aspect (emotions, mind, body, spirit) is noted on the strip beside the date, on a scale of one to five (1= very low, 5 = very high), using the five lines as the different levels. Use a colour code for each separate aspect, joining the points with a coloured pencil as you go. This will give you four coloured wave-lines on the same strip. Alongside the record, or in your journal, make brief notes of any particular energy events that seem relevant, such as 'spring-cleaned the house', 'sleepless night ' or 'excellent thinking day – paperwork sorted'.

Moon Energy Chart

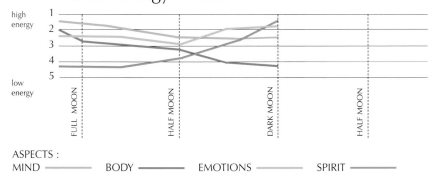

Moon chart Make a chart as described above, showing the dates of each full, half and dark moon. Many diaries will have these already marked in. Your records should extend at least four lunar cycles ahead, remembering that there are approximately thirteen cycles in a full lunar year.

Sun Energy Chart

Solar chart Make a chart as described above and mark the first day of each calendar month, as well as the quarter days, solstices and equinoxes. Make the chart for a whole calendar year to obtain the full picture, and record your energy levels on the first day of each month and at the quarter days.

Healing places

One link with the sacred land that persists around the world is the use of healing wells and springs. The sight of clear water bubbling up from the earth has a special magic and wonder, and wherever there are natural pools and springs there is the probability that the veil between the worlds will be thin. There may be accounts of spirit activity, angelic and fairy sightings in these places, and unexpected visionary experiences and inexplicable cures are often reported at natural spring sites.

When a spring has been associated with healing powers over time, it holds a powerful energy and atmosphere. There is a timeless quiet around the area and, if the spring is still visited, offerings may be left close by. Traditional gifts are flowers, food and coins, although I have also seen small votive statues, candles and photographs. In parts of Britain there are ancient well-dressing ceremonies that have originated from this custom of making offerings. The wells are decorated or 'dressed' in annual celebrations, using thousands of flower heads to create intricate patterns and pictures.

Trees can also become dwelling places for healing energies. The benefits of hugging trees are well known: the warmth of feeling and the vibrant energy that a tree can give out are quite remarkable, and when you stand in the shelter of its overhanging branches you are inside the tree's aura. Merely by sitting beneath such a tree you can benefit from its energy. Some trees have reputations as healing sites, and people may leave small gifts among their roots, or strips of 'cloutie' – cloths tied in the branches that act as prayer flags, carrying requests for healing to the powers of the winds.

Balancing energy gifts

It is important to follow the principle of fair exchange when seeking healing or other assistance from Spirit. In energy terms, if we ask to receive energy, we should offer some form of energy in return, so that all remains balanced and there is no deficit as a result of our actions. In many traditional communities this energy exchange takes the form of specific gifts, such as blankets or horses, to the healer or shaman. So if you ask for healing from the land, offer the land a gift that seems appropriate. This does not have to be left on the land, but you should inform the land what you intend; for instance, you may feel that a suitable exchange would be a cash gift to a forestry project or volunteering to spend some time working for an animal shelter.

Consulting the garden

The wise gardener saves time and energy by exploring the land's own 'medicine', how the elements are working together and what the spirits there have to say. Is the water element scarce or in abundance? It is no good planting plants that love dry, sandy soil in a waterlogged, boggy clay. Is the garden well ventilated and how does the wind move around it? Some plants cannot stand cold draughts, while others naturally thrive in exposed conditions and can give shelter to other living things. What type of soil do you have: sandy, sticky, stony, chalky? You have only to look at it and feel it to find out. Gather some earth in your hands, rub it and smell it – see if it smells sweet and fertile or sour and tired. Where is the 'fire' – the sunlight – in your garden? This is crucial information if the plants you introduce are to be happy and survive. Any of this elemental information may also explain why any plants or trees already in the garden are struggling and seem unhappy. You can consult the spirits of the garden about whether and where to move them, or how you might adjust their living conditions to help them thrive.

Leave offerings for the garden spirits: introduce yourself and ask them what they need and how you can cooperate with them. Any new plans should be discussed with them. Put temporary markers (such as short sticks) around, to map out your design plans and take time to sense the garden's response. Make time, too, to dream with the garden while your plans are forming; sit in different places – even within a small backyard – and explore with your shamanic senses and an open mind, letting ideas come to you from the garden spirits, rather than planning from gardening manuals or following the latest design fashion. When you work in cooperation with the spirits in this way, one step will lead to the next and you will benefit from the full energy of the garden spirits co-creating with you. A garden made in this way has a truly magical quality and feeds the soul.

The principle of consultation applies whether your 'garden' is a plant container on your doorstep or a large estate.

Making changes

When you have consulted your garden and decided what to plant and where, you will need to determine how and when you will begin to implement your plans. The garden spirits will offer their advice, and the many excellent manuals now available will provide other facts that you need concerning growing conditions, planting times and possible plant choices. In my own experience the process goes something like this:

Spirits: 'Put something tall for the butterflies there …'
Book: 'Buddleia and climbing roses suit these conditions.'

As with any work where advice is sought from the spirits, remember that you are in charge and ultimately it is your decision. The choices that you make should always be a matter of common sense, taking all the relevant information into account. The spirit world does not always consider human experience, and your neighbours may not be too thrilled if a highly invasive plant appears on your joint boundary.

Spirit planting

All new life begins with the dreaming stage, in Mother Earth's womb of potential. What is dreamed in potential is then birthed into matter – intention becoming reality – whether this is a plant, a child or a house. Some days before you intend to plant (whether seeds or ready-grown plants), go to the place you have chosen and start by 'planting' your intent in the sacred space, in the spot where the new plants are to grow.

1 Prepare the soil by loosening it and clearing away weeds, then add any nutrients that you feel are needed. Try to use natural feeds for the soil, such as bonemeal, compost or manure (consult your gardening book to find out what best suits the plants that are to live there).

2 For each plant place a small stone in the soil as a 'spirit seed' to announce the new arrival and call to the plant spirits that will care for it.

3 Ask for blessing and well-being for the new planting and leave a gift of smudge-herbs, or anything else that you feel is appropriate.

These 'spirit seeds' can also be used to plant changes in any setting where you are introducing something new – even for kitchen or office equipment or a new hi-fi. This process informs the harmony of what is already there of the coming changes and prepares the space so that it can integrate the 'new' more easily.

Tending and harvesting

As you keep track of the cycles of Mother Earth, the waxing and waning of the moon and the passage of the seasons, you will develop an intuitive sense about what needs to be done in your garden. By working in cooperation with the spirits you will also be getting first-hand advice about what your plant relatives need and when they need it.

Every plant has its own spirit keeper, so you can ask to meet it if a plant needs special attention. Enter the silence (see page 19), either out in the garden beside the plant or in your indoor power place, holding a small piece of the plant in question. Ask the spirit keeper for advice and put specific questions to it, such as 'Is there a disease present in this plant?' 'What should I do about it?' 'Is it likely to spread to other plants?' However, this is not a way to avoid responsibility for knowledge and learning. Sometimes garden spirits have gently reminded me to look back at my own notes of previous relevant advice that they have given me, patiently asking me to remember what I have already been told!

Each garden is individual and the balance of the energies within it is unique. This explains why, although scientific and horticultural wisdom may be followed to the letter, plants do not always behave according to the rules. A spirit-sensitive gardener will be able to grow things where they should not survive and will have a completely different approach to 'pest' control, asking insect relatives for their cooperation in the garden and accepting that all creatures have to eat and make homes. The greater the variety of wildlife that you encourage into your garden, the more the whole system will reach a state of balance, with songbirds regulating the slug population and ladybirds dealing with aphids. Moreover, plants that are happy and full of vitality are far more able to survive viral and fungal attacks and the odd chewed leaf.

Thank all the unseen and visible garden helpers regularly with your words and with heartgifts, and let them know that you appreciate their presence. If you grow food, offer the first fruits of your harvest to Mother Earth and pick only when your intuition tells you that the moment is right.

Do not be surprised if the garden speaks to you when you are going about other activities – perhaps when you are occupied indoors or walking round the supermarket. You may suddenly have a strong impulse to buy a packet of seeds or a certain plant. Once you are connected to the spirit life of your garden, your mind picks up messages and receives knowledge without deliberately 'tuning in'. It is like the communication that develops between close relatives, when they know each other's thoughts and needs on a deep, unspoken level.

Shamanic sites

You may wish to create specific sacred areas within your garden, places where you can sit and enter the silence or 'still hunt' (see page 30); somewhere to build your Medicine Wheel (see page 34); a place to dance or drum; or a hearth on which to perform the fire ceremony (see page 39). The amount of privacy and space that you have and the wishes and needs of anyone with whom you share the garden will govern whether you can set up specific shamanic sites. But you *can* create a piece of garden or a plant container that celebrates an aspect of the Web of Life that is important to you or that you are exploring and learning about at this time.

Making sacred garden features

The garden 'features' below blend easily with any setting, yet they will bestow blessings and beauty to the place and to all who visit.

- **Sun garden** A sundial tracks the path of the sun across the sky by the position of its shadow. It does not need to feature an elaborate calibrated scale marked with the hours, but could be just a simple upright stick placed where it can cast a clear shadow on the ground. You may like to mark on the ground where its shadow tip falls at the solstices and equinoxes. Use a row of pebbles or shells to make a visual record of the sun's journey at that particular time. You could decorate this area with flowers that respond strongly to the sunlight, such as daisies and sunflowers, whose 'faces' follow the sun as it crosses over them; or with flowers that have yellow, gold or red colouring in honour of the fire, such as calendulas, nasturtiums and poppies.

- **Moon garden** Position a container or round flowerbed where your plants can catch moonbeams on a clear night. Silver-leafed foliage and white flowers glow brightly in the moonlight, as do the moon-shaped seedheads of the plant known as honesty. There are both tall and dwarf varieties of evening primrose, which opens its flowers at nightfall, and many other plants that release their scent only when the light dies from the sky: night-scented stock and ornamental tobacco plants do this beautifully, inviting you out into the moonlight. You might also wish to decorate or mark out the area with white shells or stones.

- **Peace garden** Plants that evoke and symbolize peace include the thornless rose, the lotus or water lily, and other lilies of all kinds. Plant them where you can leave offerings, perhaps by a bird-feeding table or a flat stone; make a prayer arrow to place in the ground with wishes of peace for all who visit your garden from all realms, through all time. You could also include glass crystals, hanging them from decorative canes or overhanging tree branches, where they add their rainbow magic of harmony and colour throughout the year. Their sparkling is much enjoyed by the garden and by the elemental spirits.

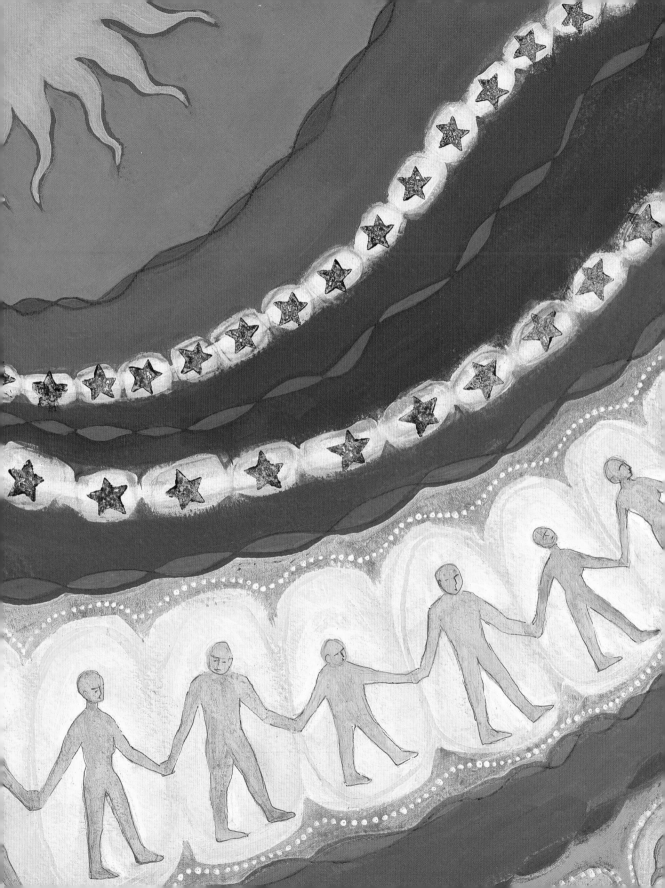

CHAPTER EIGHT
Celebrating Life

Allowing change to happen

Each new experience offers us the chance to learn and grow, and we have a choice as to whether or not we take this on willingly. For some people change feels threatening and painful, and the status quo is held onto at all costs. Every encounter with change can be seen as a 'little death', a loss of an old way of seeing the world and ourselves, and a chance to widen our experience and grow into new people. If we hold back from a succession of these opportunities for change, life often gives us a slightly firmer push from behind, with a larger and less avoidable 'little death', which may even involve personal crisis or illness. In traditional societies the major points of life-change are formalized and managed within the community through rites of passage and other ceremonials. Elders and shamans of the community or tribe are experienced in realizing when a lesson is being offered to someone – and in spotting when it is being avoided – and can help the individual to accept and go through the necessary learning with counsel, instruction, healing and ceremony.

Without this resource, we have to do our own detective work. This can be a recipe for paranoia – after all, not all that happens to us represents a lesson! But you can watch out for repeating patterns in relationships or in the challenges that you meet in your life, which may indicate that a learning experience is being offered. When we view life in this way it becomes a journey of exploration and opportunity, where even death is an ingredient of the soul's growth.

Exploring change

As we grow emotionally, physically, intellectually and spiritually we go through stages of learning that are common to human experience everywhere. If these changes are marked and witnessed by those around us, we feel better able to move on to our next phase of life. When they are not recognized or honoured, we may get stuck in old behavioural patterns, or feel unable to relate to others of our age within the community.

If you feel that you have reached a point of change in your life and wish to have a greater understanding of it, enter the silence (see page 19) or consult the Medicine Wheel (see page 34) with two separate questions: 'What is the lesson being offered to me at this time?' and 'How can I integrate this learning into my life?'

Life stages

The important transition at puberty from child to young adult has become fragmented in Western cultures into a motley collection of 'achievement' steps: graduating, learning to drive, losing one's virginity, getting promotion. These are irrelevant to the needs of this life stage, which are to end our child-dependency relationship with our parents, find out who we are as an emerging adult and be welcomed and accepted into the adult world, with respect and a place for our gifts and energy. We also need to accept new responsibilities in taking care of ourselves and playing a role in the care and upkeep of the community. In tribal communities this rite of passage is enacted through ritual and celebration, perhaps with the giving of a new name to mark the person's new status. This ceremonial crossing of the line into adulthood leaves everyone clear about the new role of the individual.

In our later years we have had enough life experience to begin to see patterns emerging, and we have enough information to know ourselves more deeply and sense our own mortality. We adjust our course towards more spiritual and inward concerns and move into the stage of eldership. But not all older people have integrated their lessons – grey hairs don't necessarily signify wisdom! At this life stage we are discovering when to speak and when to be silent, when to step in and when to hold back and let life do the teaching. We also have the experience to understand whether or not someone is ready to listen or look at things differently. In traditional cultures circles of elders support each other and the community; but often in the developed world life experience and wisdom are not valued or recognized and this is a stage where the community says older people are no longer needed. Retirement is offered as a 'reward'.

If you feel that any of these transitions are incomplete, then rites of passage – rituals that mark these transition points – can be done later on a 'catch-up' basis, and will help connect and align you with the stage in which you now find yourself. You might devise rituals with small groups of friends to celebrate and witness your new state.

Creating a rite of passage

You need to include in your ritual the following stages:

- Make a symbolic *separation* from your 'old' life, perhaps preparing beforehand by giving away items that are associated with it.
- Have a point of actual *crossing over* – anything from a cord laid on the ground to a decorated archway.
- Invite friends – some of whom should already be in your new life stage – to witness and celebrate; have them welcome you when you have crossed the line; get together with these new peers before or after the ritual, and invite them to share their experience and wisdom with you. Have a Giveaway (see page 100) or feast of celebration!

Circles of celebration

You can get great support and affirmation from working with a group of people. Gathering with others can also reinforce the intent of the group. If you are new to working in a circle and wish to get a group together, begin by inviting close family or friends to join you; having open circles – which anyone can attend – requires experience and circle-holding skills. Make sure that all who are present understand the rules for council circle where appropriate (see page 96) and the guidelines for circles shown below.

Working in a circle makes a strong container for the energy-work and shows that all are equal; and in practical terms, everyone can clearly see and hear everyone else. Here are some ideas based on rituals already covered in this book, which would be suitable circles to begin with:

- **Fire ceremony** Conduct this in the same way as described on page 39; when each person feels it is the right moment, they should approach the fire (always moving clockwise); at the West they should offer their lists to the fire and then return (still moving clockwise), coming full-circle back to their place. To finish the ceremony, pass the talking stick round in an anti-clockwise direction to give each person an opportunity to share briefly what they have experienced during the process (it is not usual to share the actual contents of the lists). This kind of sacred debriefing helps 'unwind' and ground the energy of any ceremonial circle.

- **Prayer circle** Call in the Four Directions (see page 23) and set up a Medicine Wheel or single candle in the centre of the circle. The smudge-bowl is then passed clockwise to each person in turn, allowing them to offer prayers, speaking from their heart. They should light the smudge and fan some towards the centre of the circle, allowing the smoke to carry their prayers to Spirit. To close, thank the Four Directions and blow out the candle, sending a prayer of blessing to the whole Web.

- **Earth-healing circle** With a lighted candle in the centre of the circle, enter the silence (see page 19) and visualize light and positive energy focused on the candle. Each person should focus on sending the light out into the Web as a blessing. Invite members of the circle to speak the name of any aspect of Creation that they feel called to offer for healing, so that it can be held in the light by the whole group for a moment. At the end, blow out the candle together, asking Spirit to take the light wherever it is needed.

- **Life-celebration meal** Share a sacred meal at the solstice or equinox; decorate the table and space accordingly, eat seasonal food (blessing it before beginning the meal) and take offerings out to Mother Earth with your thanks, before eating. Then enjoy!

Guidelines for circle-holding

- Smudge the space you use before and after meeting.
- Begin by asking each person to make sure their 'magic skin' is intact.
- State if the circle is confidential.
- Have a clear and simple intention for meeting and be prepared to remind the circle of it should they stray.
- Keep socializing for after the circle has been closed.

A link in time

This ritual acknowledges and celebrates our place as a link between past and future, our link with our own ancestors, and our responsibility as a living ancestor to those still to come.

You will need: smudge-kit (see page 15); fourteen night lights; one larger candle; four stones that are willing to work with you; a space large enough to enable all the candles to be set up in a line; a space to one side where you can sit.

1. Smudge yourself, the space and the items to be used. In this ritual the stones will represent the Four Directions. Decide which stone represents which Direction and place the larger candle (which represents 'you' in the ritual) in front of you, forming the centre of the line you are to build on either side.

2. Pick up the South stone and spend a few minutes reflecting on the people in your life (or your past) who are your heart-connections: lovers, friends, partners and so on. Hold the stone to your heart and let the awareness of your South/heart family be absorbed by it. Lay the stone to the South of the centre candle. Repeat the process with the North stone, reflecting on those whose thinking, mentoring, teaching and writing have influenced you. Let the stone absorb your reflection. Place it to the North of the centre candle. Repeat with the West stone, reflecting on your present bloodline family (not in-laws or step-families). Place the stone to the West of the centre candle. Repeat with the East stone, reflecting on your spirit helpers or guides and those who inspire you. Place the Stone to the East of the centre candle. The candle and the stones now reflect you as a fourfold living ancestor, as you are at this time.

3. Now place the night lights in a row: seven on each side of the centre candle. These represent the seven generations past (to the left of the centre candle) and the seven still to come (to the right). Light the candle on the far left, calling in and giving thanks for Grandfather Fire's light, balance and blessing. Now light each candle from the one before it, symbolically taking the light along the generations; include the centre candle and end at the far right. Now you can see 'your' candle as the link in this continuum of generations.

4. Make any prayers and wishes for blessing and healing that come to your heart, for yourself and for generations past and future. Sit with the lighted candles and take your time to absorb awareness of your place in this wonderful continuum of soul-learning.

5. When the process feels complete, blow out the seven 'past' candles and, as you do so, release any connection to anything in the past that does not serve your soul on this earthwalk. Blow out the seven 'future' candles, sending your love, blessings and good intent to those yet to come. Now, focusing on the centre candle, pray for yourself as a living ancestor, for balance and wisdom in your actions and choices. Blow out the candle, sending love and light to your own future path.

The way ahead

The rituals described in this book guide you through a series of sacred experiences in order to help you express a deeper connection with the sacred within life and with the Web of Life itself. If you wish to make a ritual for a specific kind of personal change, celebration or prayer, then you can adapt what is offered here or create new rituals for yourself. There is an alchemy that governs how energy and sacred space works and that goes beyond the boundaries of time, culture and geography. If we look at traditional rituals from around the world, we can see common factors in the way energy is used and in the way ritual spaces are set up.

Designing your own ritual

Here is a list of points to remember when you are creating your own ritual. It will help you with the basic alchemy and will remind you of ethical considerations.

- Keep your ritual simple – in this way it is easier for you to hold your intent and for Spirit to respond to it.
- Call in the Powers of the Four Directions for guidance, balance and protection.
- Do not call in powers or energies that are unknown to you.
- When calling to powers or energies, always add the phrase '… that love me' as a safeguard (for example, 'I call to the ancestors that love me').
- If you feel at all uncomfortable during a ritual, close down the process in an orderly way and smudge (see page 15).
- Use smudge-herbs or other means of cleansing and protecting before starting a ritual and when you have finished.
- Make sure that your aura is well protected throughout.
- Ask permission of the space and of any other relatives that will be affected and thank them afterwards.
- Have a clear and positive intent, which is neither ambiguous nor vague.
- Follow common-sense safety precautions.
- Use natural, biodegradable materials in all your work.
- Use the energy quality of the elements (for instance, the flowing of water) to match the energy of your intent.
- Do not encroach on the privacy or personal wishes of another.
- Do not manipulate the personal path or energy of another or wish them harm.
- If you are working on behalf of someone else (say, in healing work) always have their express permission beforehand.
- When asking spirits for help, remember that you have the final say – you always have a choice as to whether or not you act on their advice.
- Leave a heartgift in return for the energy and help received.

Further steps

Once you have planted the seeds of a stronger connection to the Web of Life through your intent and through ritual, the process of learning about Mother Earth and your own medicine will grow, and you may well find new connections happening as if by chance. New creatures may visit you in everyday reality, or you may sense the presence of your spirit allies at times when you need their help. The more you follow simple, enjoyable ways to connect with Mother Earth and the Web, the easier and stronger the connection will become, like the reweaving of threads.

Much information is now available about shamanism in its many aspects and in different cultural forms, and training courses in shamanic techniques are offered. Use your intuition and common sense when choosing who to study with and, if possible, work with teachers who have been established for a while and have been recommended to you. The opportunities on offer range from rain-forest pilgrimages, through workshops with tribal elders, to learning to make the shamanic journey in a central London church hall. The setting does not matter – the processes are the same. Follow your heart and your own unique path of knowledge will unfold.

If your calling is to be a shaman or healer, that path will find you. It will be a journey requiring many years of dedication and personal challenge. But you do not have to be a shaman to walk in beauty with your spirit helpers, in the company of all your relations this is a simple, natural road to travel and requires only a clear intent and an honest heart. With the map of the Medicine Wheel to guide you and help you keep your balance, there will be many wonderful discoveries along the way.

I would like to give thanks to all the creatures, stones, plants and spirit helpers that assisted me in the making of this book and to all the two-leggeds who have also helped in its production; to Grace Cheetham whose vision first called the possiblility of this book into being; toTom and Paulin for their abiding friendship and for giving me a very special place of sanctuary on the wild and elemental shores of Nolton Haven where this book could be created.

My thanks also goes to all those who have passed on teachings, and with whom I have shared circles, ceremonies and healing over the years; to Leo Rutherford for introducing me and so many others to the Medicine teachings, for his courage and integrity in bridging cultures and for his generosity of spirit; to Jonathan Horwitz for helping me deepen my shamanic practice and for his gentle clarity of teaching and service to the spirits.

I thank my children, Jeremy, Rebecca and Sofy for all we continue to learn together and for keeping my feet on the ground; to Nick for many years of companionship and learning on the Medicine Path, and for unfailing encouragement and support; to my father, who encouraged my childhood wonder of the Web, and my mother who still shows me how to learn and grow.

And to all who touch the earth with love and respect through all time.

For all my relations.

JAN MORGAN WOOD

The artwork of Jan Morgan Wood can be seen on-line at www.maytreegallery.co.uk

For information, features and contacts:
Sacred Hoop Magazine
Heddfan
Drefach Felindre
Llandysul SA44 5UH
United Kingdom
Tel: 01559 371 215
www.sacredhoop.org

For workshops and training:
Eagle's Wing
BCM Box 7475
London WC1 3XX
United Kingdom
Tel: 01435 810 233
www.shamanism.co.uk

For Shamanic training courses:
Centre for Shamanic Studies
29 Chambers Lane
London NW10 2RU
United Kingdom
Tel: 020 8459 3028
www.shamanism.dk